YOUR SPIRITUAL JOURNEY

Ancient Truths and Modern Insights

Thomas E. Legere

Foreword by Father Louis J. Cameli

LIGUORI
PUBLICATIONS

One Liguori Drive
Liguori, Missouri 63057
(314) 464-2500

Dedication

To George Maloney, S.J.

Imprimi Potest:
John F. Dowd, C.SS.R.
Provincial, St. Louis Province
Redemptorist Fathers

Imprimatur:
+ Edward J. O'Donnell
Vicar General, Archdiocese of St. Louis

ISBN 0-89243-232-2
Library of Congress Catalog Card Number: 85-50618

Copyright © 1985, Liguori Publications
Printed in U.S.A.

All rights reserved. No part of this book may be reproduced, stored in a retrieval system, or transmitted without the written permission of Liguori Publications.

Cover photo by Kristin Finnegan © 1980

Contents

Foreword by Father Louis J. Cameli 5

Introduction: Wisdom for the Whole Person 7

Part One: Beliefs

1 What's Our Secret? 11
2 Conversion 13
3 Steps Along the Way 15
4 Five Initiations 17
5 Inner Hierarchy 19
6 God's Will 21
7 Archetypes 23
8 Do Angels Really Exist? 25
9 Burning Embers 27

Part Two: Behavior

10 Heroes 31
11 My Favorite Cardinal 33
12 Christlike Behavior 35
13 Meaningful Work 37
14 Keeping Busy 39
15 Ebb and Flow 41
16 Sound Health 43
17 Introspection vs. Meditation 45

Part Three: Attitudes

18 Cosmic Humility 49
19 "Making Room" for God 51
20 Being Liked 53
21 Good, Better, Best 55
22 Being Real and Spiritual 57
23 Building the Earth 59

Part Four: Dilemmas

24 Childhood Traumas 63
25 The Problem of Evil 65
26 Spiritual Inflation 67
27 Impossible Situations 69
28 Dying to Self 71
29 True Leisure 73

Part Five: Directions

30 We're Still the One 77
31 Vows for All 79
32 Holy Russia 81
33 Science and Religion — At It Again 83
34 Physics and Spirituality 85
35 Spiritual Director 87
36 Room for All Types 89
37 Two or Three 91

Suggested Reading 93

Foreword

A very unlikely person has had a deep impact on spirituality in this century. Saint Therese of Lisieux, a young Carmelite nun who lived in a remote corner of nineteenth-century France and who died at the age of twenty-four, has shaped much of spirituality in our contemporary Church.

She taught her "little way" to God. The power of her "little way" is rooted, I believe, in the fact that it is a *little* way. She offered the world a path to God and to holiness that was accessible, available to many people. In fact, when I am trying to evaluate a form of spirituality, I often have this question in mind: Can *many* people find God and serve their brothers and sisters through this form of spirituality? Or is it reserved for a select few?

Father Tom Legere has done us all a great service in writing and sharing *Your Spiritual Journey*. Through a series of quick and spirited meditations, Father Legere opens doors to possible directions in the spiritual life. He opens doors for everyone who hears him. The spirituality he offers is not reserved for the elite. In these pages you will hear the spiritual struggle and joy of people like you and me.

Often, he opens his meditations with a question. Readers may move toward different responses; they may often move in the direction that Father Legere suggests, but sometimes they may move in another direction. No matter where you land with your conclusions, the important thing is that you find yourself awakened to the Gospel call of Jesus: "Come follow me!" It will ring in your ears with a fresh urgency.

As you finish Father Legere's meditations, perhaps you will feel the same way I did — very grateful. I was grateful for the generous ways Father Legere has shared his gifts and, above all, the great gift of his life —the Lord Jesus — with us.

May God bless the reader and the author. May we share more fully the loving mystery of God's love which comes to us as Father, Son, and Holy Spirit.

> Father Louis J. Cameli
> St. Mary of the Lake Seminary
> Mundelein, Illinois

Introduction:
Wisdom for the Whole Person

Libraries are filled with spiritual wisdom. But how many people have the time or the energy or the background to plow through the wisdom of the ages? Very few. No, most of us are content with just a few morsels of spiritual nourishment to help us make it through the day.

This book is an attempt to provide some spiritual food for a world that is starving for a word of life. What I have tried to do is to take some perennial spiritual truths (along with some current, "new age" insights) and present them in palatable fashion for people on the spiritual path.

You will not find any footnotes here, nor is there even a bibliography. Such things have their place, certainly, but I am not trying to write a heavy, scholarly treatise. I am just trying to provide some bread for the typical person on the spiritual journey.

I remember getting a tour of the Fordham University library one day. One of our teachers in the spirituality program at Fordham was helping us find our way around the library so we could use it to do serious research. Going through leather-bound tomes written in Greek and Latin, I asked myself: Who is there to translate this wisdom so that ordinary people can understand it? I resolved then and there that I would spend my energies trying to make spirituality understandable to people who take their spiritual lives seriously.

This book is an attempt in that direction. The topics are grouped into general headings having to do with our beliefs, our behavior, our attitudes, dilemmas we face along the way, and future directions for the spiritual journey. Each topic is designed to be a six-hundred-word meditation that will feed the human spirit.

The overall thrust of the meditations could best be summed up by the work "wholistic." It no longer makes any sense to talk about something being just physical or just mental or just spiritual. We now know that what happens on one level of the human person has ramifications on the other two levels.

The ancient Greeks used to say that in every person there sleeps an animal, a human, and a god. And all three must be brought to life.

The Egyptians had their symbol of the sphinx. The sphinx had the body of a lion, the head of a human, and the wings of an eagle. This was a visual aid to remind the Egyptian people that they had to learn to acknowledge and coordinate their animal nature, their human nature, and their divine nature.

This model of human wholeness has deeply captured my vision. It seems that any spirituality that is to be viable for the next century must take seriously the threefold nature of the human person.

Consequently, there are meditations included here that touch on science, psychology, and spirituality. In every instance, I have tried to show how dependent these various disciplines are on one another. Indeed, an attempt has been made to show that they are all dealing with the same Reality. It is just that each discipline represents a different path.

A word of appreciation goes to Father George Maloney, S.J., my teacher, friend, and spiritual director. He came along at a critical time in my life to help me get my bearings on the spiritual journey. This book is dedicated to him and to the message he embodies. Thanks, also, to Paula Wilson who did a great job of typing and retyping the manuscript, and to Father Louis Cameli for the kindness of his Foreword.

Part One

Beliefs

1

What's Our Secret?

A Quaker friend of mine wants to know what our secret is in the Catholic Church. The Quakers find it very difficult to get their members to come to church with any sort of regularity. We, on the other hand, continue to pack 'em in.

My Quaker friend was even more perplexed when she happened to attend Mass recently. According to her, the liturgy was a "bomb." There was no music; the priest did not even bother to preach; and he rattled the Mass off in twenty-five minutes. Yet, for some reason, you could not even get a seat in the church.

So what is our secret? With such inadequate efforts often put into planning our liturgies, why does one still have to come early to get a seat at many churches? I can think of three main reasons.

The first reason our churches are often overcrowded is that there are so darned many of us Catholics around. There are over fifty million of us in the United States. If you do not lump all Protestants together (which they rightly consider an insult), we Catholics are the largest single religious denomination in the U.S. Even with the drastic decline in attendance at Mass, we still cannot build churches fast enough. The suburban churches, in particular, are usually packed to the rafters.

The second reason that we have so many people attending Mass is that, in the past, people frequently had a lot of fear and guilt laid on them. I have never seen any statistics on this, but I am sure that many people still attend church every Sunday because they are afraid that if they do not they will burn in hell.

People with such fear will do anything to avoid missing Mass. Priests run into it often in confession. Some people insist on confessing that they missed Mass, even though they could not be there because they were sick or otherwise physically unable.

It is a disgrace to present a religion based on fear and guilt. Jesus never used those tactics. His Church should not use them either. Thank God we are moving toward a much more positive idea of religion, and fear and guilt are being used less and less. But it is still one of the reasons that some people come to Mass every Sunday.

The third reason that we do so well in getting our people out each week is the richness and power of our symbols. Back in the seminary, we were taught that the sacraments achieve their desired effect apart from the intention or the holiness of the minister. At first, this sounds like magic or superstition. But what the Church means by this is that our symbols are so powerful that the minister is secondary. We have the most ingenious collection of symbols the world has ever seen. Our symbols are time-tested ways to lead people to mental and spiritual health.

One example of such a symbol is the cross. Saint Bonaventure said that looking at the cross was the source of all his spiritual insight. There are over eighteen types of crosses used in church art. There is the Anchor, the Budded, the Celtic, the Egyptian, etc. Each type of cross is a slightly different way of expressing the coming together of the material world and the spiritual world. As an Orthodox Jewish artist recently told me, "The cross is too powerful a symbol to leave to Christians. It belongs to all of us."

Another powerful symbol is the monstrance, the showcase used for exposition of the Blessed Sacrament. Not long ago, an agnostic asked me, "Who in the heck came up with that symbol? It's ingenious." The monstrance is designed to look like the sun, leading one to focus on the Son.

We have literally scores of such symbols that are a part of the treasure-house of our faith. I am convinced that it is precisely because we have such spiritual wealth in our religious heritage that the Catholic Church will never lose its appeal.

2

Conversion

It is useless to worry about love or detachment or action or obedience or anything else, until a person goes through the process of conversion.

For many people, the word *conversion* calls to mind the process of switching from one religion to another. In its deepest meaning, however, *conversion* refers to the process whereby the individual soul returns to its Center and aligns its energies with those of the God within.

There are various levels of conversion, each one leading to more mature spiritual growth. The first level of conversion is *moral* and *ethical*. Here the soul tries to clean up its act and move from self-interest to values. This is step one. We all begin at this stage. But ethical conversion inevitably breaks down for one of two reasons. Either we discover with Saint Paul our inability to live up to the law or — something just as deadly — we actually believe that fulfilling the law will justify us.

At this point, hopefully, we step into mystery. We then begin to try to truly understand the inner nature of things. For this to take place with integrity, we need another form of conversion: *intellectual*. What this boils down to is a decision to be absolutely true to ourselves, to pursue the truth wherever it might lead us.

Here some prudence is needed. We would be absolutely foolish to ignore the guidance of the Church, since many noble souls have marched down the same road before us. But no soul has had quite the individual circumstances or insights that we have had. Cautiously, yet with integrity, we march to the beat of our own drummer.

Religious conversion comes next. This is so traumatic and bone-shattering that, while understanding it, we frequently wish we had never even begun the journey at all. It is a bit misleading to even call it an undertaking. It is more like a weak surrender.

With religious conversion we finally start to ask ourselves the questions to the answers we memorized at a more immature level of faith. Here all certainty breaks down. Nothing seems to make any sense, and life becomes unbearable. We are confronted existentially with the reality of death and the depths of our own sinfulness. This is a time of dread, bordering on despair. During this passage, people are sometimes tempted to commit suicide. The only way out is by relying on a Higher Power than ourselves.

Does everyone go through so traumatic a process? Obviously not. We all handle what we can handle and make the appropriate compromises. But for those who have been thusly tried by fire, this becomes the most important and salvific event of their lives. After being purified by the fire of love, nothing will ever again shock us. We have seen the worst in ourselves and somehow survived, so we are able to embrace a broken world compassionately.

Even though something very definite and memorable happens to us, religious conversion is not a once-and-for-all experience. We then must commit ourselves to *psychic* conversion, which entails a relentless lifetime stripping away of our illusions and delusions. We try to face ourselves daily through our dreams and our deepest thoughts. We seek healing through the Sacrament of Reconciliation and through the love of brothers and sisters in the Lord.

All of this sounds like gibberish to those who are still trying to justify themselves under the law. People who live on the surface will never understand these concluding words of Saint John of the Cross:

"Without light and apparently without strength, even seemingly without hope, we commit ourselves to an entire surrender to God. We drop our arrogance, we submit to the incomprehensible reality of our situation and we are content with it because, senseless though it may seem, it makes more sense than anything else."

3

Steps Along the Way

"When did you meet the Lord?"
"When were you saved?"
"Are you filled with the Spirit?"
People who ask questions like these have a very naïve understanding of the process of conversion. Turning to the Lord is the work of a lifetime. You just can't say you were converted last Wednesday afternoon.

Granted, there are certain moments that stand out more than others as we walk with the Lord. Certain times in our lives seem to stand out very clearly as key moments in our spiritual growth. But most of the time we move gradually along a continuum, passing certain landmarks along the way.

A lot is written about the initial conversion process, and a fair bit can be found about the "Dark Night of the Soul." But there is very little in print to help the average spiritual seeker figure out what some of the lesser-known landmarks are all about.

Sister Rose Page, writing in *Spiritual Life* magazine, lists eight stages in the total conversion process. I would like to make use of her insights while drastically simplifying them with my own wording. Her eight stages look like this:

1. Waking up. For most of our lives we believe that "what you see is what you get." It is not so much that we do not believe in the spiritual; we cannot even relate to it. Talk of the spiritual gives us the creeps. Then we have a crack in our cosmic egg. We have an experience that suggests that maybe, just maybe, there is something to it after all.

2. Taking it seriously. We decide to give this spiritual stuff a try. We pray a bit, even though we are still very self-conscious about it. We begin to read. We may "discover" the wisdom of the spiritual masters. We become intellectually convinced that we want to give this spiritual stuff an honest try.

3. Conversion. We want to make the move, but we are petrified to do so. We are almost crippled with anxiety. It suddenly dawns on us that we have gone too far to turn back. We decide to take the plunge. Pain. Relief. Exhilaration.

4. Getting — your — act — together. A lot of inconsistencies in our life present themselves. We begin to change our external behavior to make it a bit more consistent with the inner change that we now know has taken place.

5. Hanging — in — there. The good vibes that we had at the end of our conversion disappear. We start thinking that maybe we just made the whole thing up. Our prayer life dries up. Also, the old demons that we had "conquered" during our conversion present themselves again. This is a time for naked faith.

6. Real prayer. Our determination to hang in there pays off. We begin to really become believers. Prayer is not so much an activity as a backdrop for all our daily activities. We get ready to order our halos.

7. All — hell — breaks — loose. We are not sure if our prayer is really prayer at all. Maybe we are just rationalizing. This is also the time when a lot of the wild and crazy forces of our unconscious burst to the surface. The id and the superego have a field day. We feel like a cross between Hugh Hefner and Saint Alphonsus Liguori. Depression alternates with religious clarity.

8. It — was — worth — it. "I live now, not I, but Christ lives in me." The Trinity is experienced from within. People are seen as the human face of God. God is seen everywhere. We mellow out.

And then, as you might guess, the whole process begins all over again.

The distinctions between landmarks are not always so neat and clean. People experience these stages in different ways at their own pace. The one thing that all the spiritual giants seem to agree on is that the conversion process could not have begun and ended last Wednesday afternoon.

4

Five Initiations

There are five main stages — or initiations — on the spiritual path. To many, all of this will sound like a lot of gibberish. But those who have begun the spiritual journey in earnest will know exactly what is being spoken about.

The *first stage* is the experience of being "born again." This term rubs some people the wrong way because they think it is used only by charismatics. But the first one to use the term was Jesus. This "second birth" is fundamental to a life in the Spirit. All the great religions of the world speak about such an experience or one parallel to it. It is no less than the discovery of the God within. Until this happens we are still beautiful people, loved unconditionally by God, but we do not have a clue as to what the spiritual journey is all about.

Once we have awakened to the fact that, as Jesus says, "the kingdom of heaven is within" us, we now enter a very pivotal *second stage*. We wake up to our own latent spiritual powers, and we must decide how these powers will be used. We can choose to become a monster or a lover. We can use our spiritual power to manipulate, like the Reverend Jim Jones, or to serve, like Dorothy Day.

If we choose to serve, then we find ourselves cast in the role of teacher. People come to us to be fed, not because we have it all together, but because we have a treasure within our weak, earthen vessels.

The *third stage* leads the disciple into a greater intimacy with the Lord and the saints. Spiritual questions are answered, and the disciple experiences his or her "no-thing-ness." Along with Jesus, the disciple says, "I and the Father are one."

For some strange reason, any "triumph" is always followed by an ordeal. The disciple begins to sense that the spiritual journey, with all of its joy and illumination, inevitably leads one to Calvary.

In the *fourth stage* of the journey, Calvary becomes a reality. There is agony in the garden when the disciple is tempted to give up the spiritual path. One is betrayed and denied by friends and those who should know better. One is mocked for one's interest in the spiritual path. One is stripped of all securities. In a moment of seeming abandonment even by God, the disciple appears to have been defeated. While crying out to God from a position of near despair, the soul sinks all the way to the depths of hell.

Like Jesus, however, the Father raises to life the soul that has been tested and purified. In this *fifth stage*, the disciple comes back to teach others what he or she has experienced. The tested disciple is confident without being cocky, self-assured without being arrogant, and patient without being passive.

Obviously, nobody ever told us about all this when we were studying the *Baltimore Catechism*. We were taught a very cut-and-dried form of religion. That is why Catholics who have a firsthand encounter with the living God sometimes get thrown for a loop. They think that their religious insight may be leading them to join some other movement or religion. Everywhere you go these days, you run into Catholics who have decided, for one reason or the other, to move on to "greener pastures."

The pity about this is that our spirituality is second to none. In fact, when Protestants are interested in deeper prayer experiences they almost invariably turn to the Catholic saints and mystics.

The spiritual journey is filled with surprises. And perhaps the biggest surprise of all is that the journey is not really a journey at all. We simply get in touch with who we always were in the mind of God.

5

Inner Hierarchy

Everything, absolutely everything, about authentic religion has a deeper, inner meaning. This applies even to the notion of hierarchy. While most people think of the hierarchy only as a group of individuals engaged in Church leadership, the deepest meaning of the hierarchy is that it is a symbol of the various levels of our own soul transformation.

We begin the spiritual path as seekers. We try this, and we try that. We read the latest "in" spiritual writers; we listen to a tape by a popular guru; we dabble with TM or some consciousness-raising group. We might even investigate everything from numerology to Tarot cards. We have intensity but no real commitment yet to a particular path or Savior.

If we are lucky, the living God meets us on our path, and we fall flat on our faces in adoration. We are at least partially converted to the Lord. Not that we are perfect or make any pretenses to having it all together, but we are at peace in calling ourselves followers of Jesus Christ.

At this point we are *spiritually* ordained as *priests*. A priest does not necessarily possess personal holiness; a priest is someone who celebrates the symbolic, sacramental presence and power of the Lord. A priest also plumbs the depths of the Scriptures and is responsible for translating the Word into daily life. Spiritually, we try to do the same thing.

By virtue of his specific responsibilities, a priest has a somewhat limited scope and vision. It is the job of the *bishop* to be looking after the big picture. We become a bishop, spiritually, when we are no longer concerned with just following the rules of the Christian path, but when we begin to see the bigger spiritual picture. We read the Gospels with a deeper meaning. We see the plan of God unfolding in the Church and in the world, even while no one else sees it. We become more tolerant of our own human weaknesses because we see the presence and the power of Christ dwarfing our human failings.

An *archbishop* usually has an even larger scope than a normal bishop. He, at least theoretically, oversees a large geographical area composed of several different dioceses. We become archbishops, spiritually, when our ability to see Christ extends into areas beyond local Church interests. We think globally, not parochially. We notice trends within ourselves and within our world, and we ask ourselves, What is God trying to tell me by this event? Our interest expands into areas of social justice, science, psychology, even economics. Everywhere we see the superimposed figure of the risen Christ growing and growing as he stretches his arms out to embrace the cosmos.

The Holy Father dares to speak to us in the name of Christ. When this archetypal dimension is touched off in our psyches, we begin to tremble in awe. For we realize that we are not called to do just the things of God (like the priest) or to discern the plan of God (like the bishop) or to look for God in the larger context of the world (like the archbishop). We are actually called to be other Christs. We are called to speak and think and act in the name of Him whom we follow.

During this whole journey, it is not the ego that is growing in stature. Otherwise, it would be a demonic trip, based on the greatest illusion. No, it is our True Self, our Higher Self, our God-self, our Christ-self, that is gradually growing inside of us by God's grace.

A further word of caution:

The spiritual journey happens within us. We may hold the external office of priest but, internally, still be a seeker. Or internally we may still think of ourself as a seeker, yet be more in contact with our God-self than we realize.

6

God's Will

One of the biggest questions for people journeying in the Spirit is how they can figure out God's will for themselves. Here I will attempt to offer a few simple guidelines.

First of all, even though anything is possible with God, we do not usually get God's communication to us in a sudden or dramatic fashion. A voice does not ring from the heavens with a clear-cut set of instructions to us. In fact, God does not even usually offer us concrete signs.

So, how does God speak to us? The process is very simple: God whispers in our hearts. As we cut off the external noise and the internal dialogue, we begin to move below the surface of life. We go deeper than social roles and conventions. We go deeper than rules and laws.

We approach what T. S. Eliot called "the still point of the turning world"; and there, in the deepest recesses of our heart, we get a sense, a feel, an intuition of where we should go and what we should do.

Whoa, wait a minute. Won't such an approach lead to moral anarchy? Won't this open the gates to everyone irresponsibly "doing their own thing"?

That, apparently, was what the officials of the Inquisition thought when they hauled in Ignatius of Loyola, the founder of the Jesuits, to appear before that august body. They accused Ignatius of advocating "private revelation" from God.

Ignatius was apparently a lot wiser than his inquisitors. He refused to back down and demonstrated that his position is the authentic Catholic teaching on the matter.

While the possibility of self-delusion is always right around the corner, nevertheless it must be stubbornly maintained that God is always free to communicate with us in a personal way. In addition, when people get in touch with their deepest selves, they can usually trust themselves.

The process of discernment is, of course, absolutely necessary to help us figure out when we are truly on the right track. The Jesuits, because of their strong belief in personal communication between God and human beings, have worked out the most sophisticated thoughts on discernment that we have today.

So, even though proper discernment is an absolute necessity, the point here is that God can and does communicate in a personal way with individuals.

What is the role of the Church in this process of personal discernment? It is the Church's responsibility to decide how to best use the person's private revelation. Church authority is supposed to coordinate and harmonize the various individual charisms and prayerful insights of individuals.

As one can imagine, this is seldom a smooth process. Individuals feel called to move in a certain direction; Church authorities do not always agree.

While Church authorities have an absolute right to decide what is best for the overall functioning of the Church, they have no right to claim that they always know what God's will is. Sometimes the individual may be doing exactly what God wants. It is just that the person cannot convince Church authorities that *this* is what God wants.

The annals of the Church are literally filled with such prophets who were years ahead of their time. Ignatius of Loyola, Teresa of Avila, Catherine of Siena, Francis of Assisi, Thomas Merton, and Teilhard de Chardin are a few of the better-known ones who were constantly in hot water for their visionary ideas.

As can be seen, discerning God's will is a very tricky process. Ultimately, whether the individual is right or the Church is right, only God knows.

7

Archetypes

What in the heck is an archetype? Very simply, it is a spiritual pattern that is found in the mind. We are not consciously aware of our archetypes; so they manifest themselves in symbolic images occurring in dreams, fantasies, myths, poetry, art, religion, and nature.

Some examples of common archetypes are gods and goddesses, witches and devils, the sky, the earth, the sea, the mountains, the vine, the tree, the cross, the circle, mother, father, mate.

What makes an archetype so special are two things: one, its origin and two, its universality. Let us examine these components one at a time.

Where do archetypes come from? No one seems to know. But one thing is for certain: they go back a long, long time. In fact, the first part of the term comes from the Greek word *arche*, which means beginning. The clear suggestion, then, is that archetypes were present in the minds of people from the very beginning of time.

The second intriguing aspect of archetypes has to do with their universality. Identical spiritual patterns, with some minor cultural variations, seem to be present in all peoples, in all civilizations, on all continents.

By now you may be asking yourself, Where did these spiritual patterns come from? Who put them there? Because no one is able to trace their origins and because they keep popping up with amazing regularity in all cultures, there are only two possible answers that seem credible. One answer is that certain spiritual leaders all had the same insights and passed them on with such regularity that they eventually became embedded in the human psyche. The other answer is: they came from a Higher Source.

The first possibility raises more questions than it answers. For example, what about all the tribes and civilizations that have not had any contact with other peoples for thousands of years? Isn't it reasonable to conclude that at least somewhere along the line someone would have neglected to pass on these truths? What are the odds that the aborigines, the Aztecs, and the Africans all were taught the same spiritual truths at the same time? The odds are not very good.

This brings us to the possibility that a Higher Source imbued and embedded these spiritual patterns in our brains from the beginning of the human race up until the present. That is what I personally believe, but that is only my belief. That does not prove anything to anyone.

Enter Carl Jung who put a clever twist on the question. His point was that it is futile to argue how these archetypes got in our minds. The point is that whether we think their origin is human or divine we still have to deal with them. Jung would put it this way: "We all have to act *as if* the archetypes are true, so why waste our effort trying to figure out where they come from? For good mental health we must accept them as a fact of life and deal with them accordingly."

For a generation beset with doubts, Jung's argument makes a lot of sense. For example, let us take the "God" archetype. Jung found that all people are born with such an archetype. He would say: "Just accept the fact that you will have to act at least *as if* God exists if you want to strive for mental health. Don't bend your mind trying to solve the unsolvable. Just go with this basic spiritual pattern that you were born with."

So, the next time you are at a cocktail party, remember that the latest spiritual buzz word to use is "archetype." It is an idea so profound that it is actually simple.

8

Do Angels Really Exist?

If you want to cause a few raised eyebrows at your next cocktail party, try announcing to your friends that you believe in angels. You will be lucky if your friends only raise their eyebrows. They may well call the men in the white coats.

Why is there such resistance to belief in these spiritual beings that used to be such an integral part of Catholic spirituality? Very simply, we have all been brainwashed into thinking that nothing is real unless it can be measured. This actually is what it means to be a materialist. A materialist is not just someone who is obsessed by the pursuit of material objects — although it means that, too. A materialist is also anyone who does not believe a thing is real unless it can be seen, touched, heard, or smelled.

The spiritual tradition, on the other hand, has always insisted that there are levels of reality not ordinarily accessible to our waking consciousness. When one is in an altered state of consciousness (as can happen in prayer or meditation or during ritual), one can gain access to these other vibrational planes. And when one does, one encounters spiritual beings that are as real as you or I.

At this point, let us be clear that the existence of these spiritual beings is explicitly stated in the Hebrew-Christian Scriptures. There is not just an oblique reference or two; it runs all through the Bible. Of the seventy-two books of the Bible, thirty-five of them contain explicit references to angels.

Nor is this just a phenomenon peculiar to the Old Testament. Angels are present at the Incarnation, the Nativity, the Temptation in the Desert, Gethsemane, the Resurrection, and the Ascension. Angels appear to the apostles in the Acts of the Apostles, and John speaks of them in the Book of Revelation.

Furthermore, our great mystics report contact with these discarnate spirits. Augustine, Francis of Assisi, Teresa of Avila, and Bernard are a few among many who had firsthand contact with these beings.

I would suggest, then, that if one wanted to eliminate belief in angels from Christianity one would have to radically revise the Scriptures as well as our mystical tradition.

So much for the past. But why do people no longer experience these beings in modern times? The fact is that some people still do. But they keep quiet about their experiences because they do not need the aggravation of having to prove their own sanity.

A Catholic mystic told me that he is aware of two great angels who flank the altar during Mass. Their presence is as real to him as the people in his pew. This man is not a schizophrenic. He has a Ph.D. and is a highly successful businessman.

Another man told me of an experience that he had had with angels. While flying home from a business trip, he saw his father pass by the window of his plane escorted by two beings whom he did not recognize. When he arrived at his destination, his wife met him and said, "I have some bad news for you." He said, "I know, my father died." She asked, "How did you know?" He replied, "You'd never believe it."

OK, so maybe they exist. But what do angels have to do with my life? Part of the teaching of the Church has been that these spiritual entities wish to help us on our spiritual journeys. A guardian angel — or "spirit guide," if that is less of a turn-off to you — is assigned to us at our baptism. Its job is to lead us to the Truth and to keep us from harm.

Our grossly materialistic world is just now getting to believe in extraterrestrial beings. Maybe we will also be able to make room for beings who dwell on a different plane besides the physical.

9

Burning Embers

Why are people so fascinated by an open fire? From the days of our ancestors who lived in caves until the present, people have always loved to just sit and stare at fire and wood doing their thing together.

Saint John of the Cross, one of our most famous Christian mystics, says that what happens to fire and wood is exactly what happens when we and God interact.

God is the fire, and we are the log. Before being thrown into the fire, the log has its own identity. The log may be young and unseasoned, or it may be aged just right. Whatever, the point here is that it is not yet in the fire.

This situation corresponds to the stage where the ego and God are entirely separate. This separation may manifest itself in open rebellion to God or, more subtly, a belief that God is "out there." In any event, the log still sits comfortably away from the all-consuming flames.

One day, abruptly, the log is thrown into the fire. Does anyone really, consciously, choose to step into the mystery of God? Some do, I am sure. But most of us find ourselves thrown into the fire by the circumstances of life. Given a choice, we would much rather have tried to keep God at bay.

Once thrown onto the fire, the log does not immediately become one with the flames. First of all, a lot of impurities have to be burned away. The log may be moist. The log may be dirty. The log may have termites. Before the log really becomes a part of the fire, a lot of stuff has to go.

When we are first cast onto the fire of God's all-consuming love, we too have to drop a lot of stuff before we become a burning ember. We have to face our "shadow" — the dark part of ourselves. We have to face our past. We have to take a good look at the illusions and delusions we have about ourselves. We must come face-to-face with our pride and accept our own limitations.

None of this is any fun. The log is still a log. We have not yet joined the fire, and the flames are uncomfortable. We feel like we are being destroyed rather than transformed.

It gets worse. The moisture and impurities have been burned away, but we are still not a part of the flames. As John of the Cross puts it, the fire "gradually turns the wood black, makes it dark and ugly, and even causes it to emit a bad odor."

We may feel like God's love has destroyed us. What makes it worse is that we do not even see what is happening as being God's love at all. We just feel like we have been stripped naked by life, and we may wish with all our heart that we had been allowed to stay on the woodpile.

A person who has been thrown onto the fire of God's love is never the same again. The person is no longer "under the Law," is not afraid of criticism or even death. The inner freedom the person possesses is amazing.

The price such a person must pay is, of course, the utter transformation of the ego. People who have paid such a price and have gone through such a journey are the greatest resource of the human race.

So, the next time you are seated before an open hearth, throw another log on the fire and think of the journey we are called to undergo.

Part Two

Behavior

10

Heroes

At first glance, it would seem that we live in the age of the antihero. For the first time in recorded history, we seem to look up to absolutely no one.

All civilizations have always had their heroes. The United States is no exception. Our first heroes were the cowboys and frontiersmen. People admired the rough, tough men and women who first settled this country.

True cowboys have practically disappeared. Urban cowboys with thousand-dollar boots try to keep the myth going, but it no longer turns us on the way it once did.

Our next set of heroes were the military. Brave soldiers with their dashing exploits and hand-to-hand combat have provided plots for hundreds of movies during the last fifty years.

But the military no longer turns us on anymore, either. How can one admire Doctor Strangeloves who are talking about "winnable" nuclear wars? How can we be inspired by requests to start preparing for germ warfare? It is insanity.

More recent heroes were those in the political arena. We admired the suffragettes and the civil rights leaders and all those working for a better society.

Today, instead, we are witnessing the debunking of political leaders. Each year we find out that this or that president had a mistress, that "money talks," and that judicial favors can be bought.

Finally, we have even become disillusioned with our athletes. As a young boy, I practically worshiped professional athletes — *all* professional athletes. I remember how excited I was the time I got the autographs of Chico Fernandez, Solly Hemus, and Ron Northey! Today, of course, we are all aware that many professional athletes play not for love of the sport but for money.

As painful as the dethroning of our heroes has been, it seems to me that it was an inevitable process. God is now calling forth a new type of hero, the spiritual journeyer. We have explored the entire globe and have made it to the moon. The next step in our evolution is to develop the human spirit. I predict that those who advance our consciousness as a human race will be admired every bit as much as our heroes of the past.

Developing consciousness can be done in either an inner-directed or an outer-directed fashion. An example of the inner-directed hero is Thomas Merton. He is the very epitome of the spiritual searcher. He went from Quakerism to agnosticism to Hinduism to Roman Catholicism to an openness to Buddhism. Even though it would have been the last thing he ever wanted to happen (a good sign), Merton is being cast in the role of a contemporary hero. Along with Teilhard de Chardin, Merton was one of the true pivotal thinkers of our day, a genuine hero of consciousness.

Some are more outer-directed than Merton. Two such individuals are Pope John Paul II and Mother Teresa. Although both have a mystical side to them, they are known primarily for their service to the human race. Most polls indicate that they are among the most admired people of our day.

A more controversial figure for our times is Daniel Berrigan, S.J. He is brilliant, articulate, prayerful, and completely consistent in his opposition to war, especially nuclear war. It is clear by now that he is not a "flake." Even those who disagree with his methods are amazed at his consistency and his willingness to pay any price for his vision.

This, then, is not the age of the antihero at all. We just have different criteria today. This development is one more indication that we are making progress in the spiritualization of the planet.

11

My Favorite Cardinal

Imagine the impact on the United States of America if atheist Madalyn Murray O'Hair suddenly announced she was going to become a Roman Catholic. That is how shocked England was when John Newman left the Anglican faith to become a Catholic.

Controversy was to become John Newman's middle name. He was labeled a traitor by the Anglicans and a heretic by the right-wingers in the Catholic Church. He lived his eighty-nine years always in the eye of the hurricane, yet always with great inner peace.

In his youth Newman had been a brilliant teacher at Oxford. Ordained an Anglican priest at age twenty-four, he succeeded in outflanking and outreasoning Catholic intellectuals. But, gradually, Newman began to speak persuasively of the need for the Anglicans to unite themselves with Rome. His "progressive" ideas brought him a censure by twenty-four Anglican bishops as well as his peers at Oxford.

At age forty-two he resigned from the Anglican priesthood after preaching a sermon on "The Parting of Friends." After two years of further personal inquiry, Newman eventually joined the Catholic Church and began studies for the priesthood.

He was sent for his seminary studies to Propaganda Fide University (my old alma mater) in Rome. In his "autobiography" he mentions how amused he was as a student to be sitting in class while some of his professors spoke about the heretical ideas of that Anglican, John Newman.

Newman eventually became the champion of Catholic intellectuals and, conversely, the archenemy of conservative terrorists. While editor of the *Rambler*, he wrote an article on the need to consult the faithful in matters of doctrine. Although his ideas were quite orthodox, this article cost him his job and marked the real beginning of his harassment by right-wingers in the Church. A letter each day arrived at the Holy Office, accusing him of all kinds of unorthodoxy. He was a person who, like practically all of our saints, was completely misunderstood in his time.

Newman, of course, continued to think and continued to write. He believed in papal infallibility, but he was against making it a defined Catholic doctrine. Much to the consternation of the archconservatives, he was invited to the First Vatican Council (1869-1870) as an "expert" by Pope Pius IX. Newman begged off, however, realizing he would not be welcome and that his ideas would be misinterpreted. He preferred to stay in England and continue his life of prayer.

At the conclusion of Vatican I, Newman predicted its work would be completed by another Council dealing with collegiality — the sharing of authority in the Church. His prediction proved prophetic; in our time Vatican II (1962-1965) has spoken of the need for collegiality at all levels of decision-making in the Church.

Out of the blue, after Vatican I, Pope Leo XIII (1878-1903) surprised everyone by raising Newman from a simple priest to a cardinal. Newman was seventy-six years of age at the time. He did not want this honor, but Leo persuaded him to take it as a sign that the Church had a place, after all, for real intellectuals.

Newman accepted the title only so that the respectability of the Catholic Church would be enhanced in intellectual circles. He refused to wear the "cota" (the thirty-three-foot-long train that cardinals used to wear) and rejected all the pomp and hoopla that often surround the hierarchy.

Up until this time, Newman had suffered greatly. He had been the innocent victim of a scurrilous smear campaign. However, for the good of the Church, he never publicly defended himself against the criticism that came his way.

Even in death he continues to be controversial. We have Newman Centers on most of our secular university campuses; the man is quoted often as a theologian, a poet, and a visionary. Yet, he has never been officially canonized. If John Newman is not in heaven, however, I'm not sure I want to be there.

12

Christlike Behavior

I would not recommend Christlike behavior for anyone. Jesuslike behavior, certainly. But not Christlike. Let me explain.

The term "Christlike behavior" has come to mean being Godlike — in other words, consistent, without flaw, and utterly beyond the feeling level. The only problem with that is that we are human beings. We are not, nor are we expected to be, perfect.

Some people try, though. They strive to be "other Christs" or to "behave in a Christlike manner." So, when they inevitably fall flat on their faces or have a moral lapse or lose their temper, they begin the process of self-recrimination and self-hatred.

The funny thing is that Jesus did not behave in a Christlike fashion, at least according to the above understanding of the term. That is one of the reasons why he is so attractive to us. We can relate to him. Jesus cried at the death of Lazarus, got angry at the Pharisees, totally lost his temper with the money changers in the Temple, got depressed at the failure of the Jews to recognize God's plan, and even questioned God's will by asking, "My God, my God, why have you forsaken me?"

By focusing on the Jesus of the Gospels, we can get the courage to accept ourselves as we are. We can strip away the illusion of ever being Godlike. It is hard enough trying to be a decent human being.

According to Dr. Theodore Rubin, there are lots of illusions that we have about ourselves. Besides the one about being Christlike, we also have grandiose illusions involving mastery, perfection, bravery, courage, omniscience, omnipotence, great virtuosity, and invincibility. In addition, we aggrandize ourselves through illusions of being martyred, benevolent, abused, self-sacrificing, pure, saintly, understanding, all-loving, all-caring, being the eternal nice guy, entirely free of jealousy, hypocrisy, envy, duplicity, possessiveness, and dishonesty.

All of these illusions are, of course, self-defeating. They contribute to alienation from ourselves as we actually are.

We all seem to have our own list of illusions. Dr. Albert Ellis has some great ones. Here are a few of my favorites from him:

1. It is a dire necessity for an adult human being to be loved or approved of by virtually every other significant person in his or her community.

2. One should be thoroughly competent, adequate, and achieving in all possible respects if one is to consider oneself worthwhile.

3. One should become quite upset over other people's problems and disturbances.

4. There is invariably a right, precise, and perfect solution to human problems, and it is catastrophic if this perfect solution is not found.

5. Human happiness is externally caused, and people have little or no ability to control their sorrows and disturbances.

It is amazing how many illusions we have about ourselves. Thomas Merton said that the spiritual life has as its chief aim the stripping away of our illusions and delusions.

As varied as all of the illusions are, it seems to me that they are all variations of pride. We refuse to let God be all in all. We want to be something independent of God. It is the Garden of Eden all over again.

We want to be perfect, without flaw or blemish. We strive to be angels, and reject our own humanity in the process.

A few years ago I wrote a column on "Perfectionism" that got me more mail than I have ever received about anything that I have ever written. Apparently, there are a lot of folks who are spending much of their energy fighting themselves. Why not give ourselves the wonderful gift of self-acceptance? We are allowed, you know.

13

Meaningful Work

Contrary to public opinion, people do not work just because they have to. It is part of people's nature to use their brains and their hands to dig into the human enterprise. And why not? God so loved the world that he sent his only Son. If the Father thinks the world to be so worthwhile, it is only natural that we, too, should take it seriously and immerse ourselves in it.

The Father did not create the world as a finished product. New things are happening all the time. It is our job to realize our dignity as God's co-creators and to love the world as much as God does. Our goal is to reflect back to the Father a grateful, loving, and just world.

All of this is good in theory; but, unfortunately, many workers do not look on their contribution this way. They regard their jobs as a way to make a buck, no more and no less. Many factory workers simply find their work to be boring, monotonous, and dehumanizing. They come to resent their work, even stooping to deliberate sabotage of products as a way of expressing their anger at the system.

Those who are fairly well-off and employed in relatively meaningful work can't understand why the blue-collar workers are dissatisfied. After all, they are getting paid for their work, and if they don't like it they can always quit.

Such thinking, of course, begs the question. Sure, the men and women can quit, but they hang in there because they love their families and they have bills to pay. You have to admire their self-sacrifice. Any sensitive individual will be upset with a system that has people spending one-third of their lives doing something they despise just so they can continue to survive.

The Church can help blue-collar workers in a couple of ways. First, we can continue to support workers' rights to unionize and demand decent working conditions. Any spirituality of work that sidesteps the need for social reform is obscene.

However, once we have raised our voices in protest and put our resources on the line, we can also help people to cope. We can say more, much more, about the value of work done in love.

The Hindus teach that a meal cooked without love is poison. The same applies to anything we do. If it is done with a spirit of resentment, it can sour our disposition and end up being counter-productive. It is not so much what we do that matters, but how we do it. Any action done out of love can be redemptive.

I think of Brother David Steindl-Rast, one of the leaders in spiritual renewal in the United States. When not on the road, he is known back at the monastery as "Brother Cook." He mentioned to a group of us that when he is preparing a meal for his brothers, he tries to do so with as much reverence as a priest saying Mass. He said that, for him, his kitchen table is his altar.

Consciously doing something out of love changes the nature of the activity entirely. Lately, I have spent the final minute before celebrating Mass not thinking of my homily, as I used to do, but just loving the people in church. As Father John Powell says, performances never move hearts; only love does.

What we do should flow from who we are. The Church should continue to back up people who think that way. And, in the meantime, it can remind us that anything we do out of love is nothing less than Jesus continuing to touch the world he loves so much.

14

Keeping Busy

In this society everyone seems to admire a person who keeps busy. Conversely, people of a more contemplative nature are frequently considered to be lazy and nonproductive.

A lot of this kind of thinking goes back to the old adage we heard as youngsters: "An idle mind is the devil's workshop."

It is true that people who spend time in solitude do meet their inner devils. But they also meet the God within. People who are always busy, on the other hand, encounter neither the demonic nor the divine. That is why they are so shallow.

Busy people may be interested in genuinely serving humankind. It is more likely, however, that they are just trying to run away from themselves. They are desperately afraid that if the pace ever slows down, they will have to take a good look at themselves. So, they keep on pushing.

Keeping busy is a kind of narcotic. It is like taking drugs or alcohol. It is more popular than drugs or alcohol, however, because it is considered socially acceptable. One of the things I am convinced of is that no real spiritual growth is possible until we slow down.

All of the great figures from history have had a contemplative side to them. Think of Jesus, and then the Buddha, Mohammed, Confucius, Augustine, Merton, de Chardin, Einstein, and countless others — all individuals who spent a lot of time thinking and working on themselves.

Jesus, in particular, was committed to spending time in solitude. First of all, he spent thirty of his thirty-three years in almost total obscurity. And during the three years he spent in public life, it seems that half of the time nobody knew where he was. When they eventually tracked him down, he was in the desert or on a mountaintop or out in a boat or visiting his personal friends in Bethany.

Many people find it almost impossible to say "No." They want to do the Christlike thing. Well, apparently the Christlike thing is to be frequently unavailable.

Why? Was Jesus selfish? Just the opposite. Jesus knew that he would have nothing to give people if he did not first of all know who he was. So, he spent lots of time finding out.

Jesus was the Messiah, but apparently he did not have a "messiah complex" like a lot of us do. If Jesus gave top priority to taking care of his own needs, perhaps he was trying to teach us something. If we were humble enough, we would not take ourselves so seriously.

A person who seems to have understood this lesson was Swiss psychologist Carl Jung. Jung was an extremely busy counselor and prolific writer, but he would take one month off out of every four. He felt he needed the time to allow the negativity that he had absorbed from others to be washed away. There is something in the American psyche that looks askance at such a life-style. Deep down many of us suspect that Jung was just goofing off.

During one very busy time in his life, Jung told a woman that he could not see her that week because his schedule was booked up. While sailing on Lake Zurich, the woman happened to drift past Jung's lakeside home, and she spotted him sitting by the lake with his feet in the water. The next time she saw Jung, the woman upbraided him for not telling her the truth. Jung replied: "No, I had an appointment with myself, one of the most important ones I ever have."

We live in a crazy society of ulcers, heart attacks, and migraine headaches. But what is the point of it all? What are we trying to prove? Let us pray for the humility of people like Jesus and Carl Jung. Let's slow down and let God be God.

15

Ebb and Flow

In all of life there is the principle of ebb and flow. There is a time for action and a time to rest, a time to give and a time to receive.

Wise is the person who learns how to balance the ebb and the flow of God's energy. We receive God's energy in prayer, in reading, in communing with nature, in being ministered to by family and friends, in being educated, and by resting. We transmit God's energy in creativity and in loving service.

An image to help us understand this spiritual law of the ebb and the flow of things is a blood pressure test. When we have our blood pressure taken, two things are measured: the amount of pressure registered when the heart is pumping blood through the arteries (diastolic) and the amount of pressure registered in between beats (systolic). In a healthy person the diastolic rate is slightly higher than the systolic rate. Both the ebb and the flow are necessary, but our flow ideally is a little greater than our ebb. We should always be receiving a bit more than we are giving.

If we get this rhythm out of balance, we will either be giving off the exact same amount we receive or we will actually be giving off more than we receive. In the case where we receive and give the same amount, we are like a mere conduit for God's energy; the energy passes through as fast as it is received. The danger here is that we have no reserve tank, no surplus. In a case of emergency or in a period of extraordinary demands being made on us, we can run completely out of gas and stall out.

Then, there is the final case where the outcome is obvious. If we are consistently giving out more than we receive, we completely burn out and are no good to anyone.

The image I like best is that of a cup overflowing. People are constantly being fed from our overflow while we always try to keep our cup filled with God's energy. In an emergency, we can usually respond without seriously depleting our reserves.

The only one who seems to have maintained this balance perfectly was Jesus. For thirty years he filled up his cup; and then, during his three years of public ministry, he still made time to be off somewhere in the desert or on the lake or on a mountaintop getting recharged with driving energies. Most of us do not usually do as well as Jesus. We easily get things out of balance.

A priest friend of mine is an example of a beautiful person whose toughest challenge seems to be keeping a balance between the ebb and the flow of life. His priesthood has fallen into a pattern. He gives himself and gives himself for five years or so, and then he has a breakdown. After six months or so of recuperation, he is back on the job for another five years until the same imbalance catches up with him again.

When we look at the big picture and view things from the perspective of millions of years, I suppose it is not all that important whether a person is a sprinter or a long-distance runner. The number of years we live and the pace at which we work are not, ultimately, all that significant. A person who breaks down every so often because of imbalances in life-style is loved just as much by God as anyone else.

The ebb and the flow of our lives are important for what they may say about who we ultimately depend on. The person who seems to be always giving, always on-the-go, and self-denying may just be expressing a desperate need to be approved by others. On the other hand, the person who does not take self too seriously, who knows how to relax, and who loves to be loved may actually be the one who is more in tune with God's plan for human beings.

16

"Sound" Health

Without music, life would be impossible. Not just because music is pleasing to the ear but because all of life *is* music. Let me explain.

Modern-day physics tells us that everything is energy. Nothing is "solid"; all things are composed essentially of light waves. Now we are discovering that these light waves have a vibrational quality to them. In other words, everything we see around us — including people — consists of vibrational tones (music) that has taken on form.

If this is true, then the human organism is a kind of musical instrument. It can be positively or negatively affected by various vibrations. Good music can make it feel better, while discordant music can actually make it physically sick.

I remember the first time I became aware that vibrations had a "shape" to them. It was at the beginning of Walt Disney's classic film, *Fantasia*. Do you remember how the film showed the various patterns caused by the different musical instruments?

Every sound that is around us is actually doing something to our bodies. The whirr of a refrigerator, the bark of a dog, the blare of sirens, the honk of car horns — all of these sounds are influencing our health. It has been demonstrated, for example, that the beat employed by most rock groups (long-short-short) actually weakens a person's physical strength. This effect takes place, apparently, whether or not one actually "likes" the music. In other words, the human organism is thrown out of "sync" just by being exposed to groups like the Rolling Stones.

Classical music is so powerful because it tries to bring out the best in people. We even have to watch out here, however. Some classical music is designed to stimulate our sex drive. (Listen to "Tristan and Isolde" sometime.) And some classical music appeals to our power drive. (After listening to Wagner, Hitler's favorite composer, one feels like going out and conquering the world.)

It seems to me that the best thing we can do for the human organism in this regard is to expose ourselves to good "New Age" music and good liturgical music.

"New Age" music has as its starting point a conscious realization that the human organism is a musical instrument. It considers the various energy centers within the human body, and chooses the precise sound and the precise musical instrument to stimulate the body in the proper way.

The acknowledged leader in this field is Steve Halpern, Ph.D., who has made it his life's work to develop music that literally heals people on both an emotional and a physical level.

Good liturgical music was written without benefit of the insights of modern-day physics, but it appears to be right on target. This is true especially of Latin hymns and chants. Whether or not people understood the words is immaterial. What is important is that the sounds of the Latin language actually affect people in a positive physical way.

To get a sense of this, put your hand over your heart and chant "Ah-men." Now do the same with the Sanskrit chant "Om." Both chants stimulate the heart center, an energy center that was very important to Jesus.

If sound is capable of affecting us in such profound ways, then it becomes our responsibility to exercise some control over the sounds we expose ourselves to. There is more truth than ever to the dictum, "A sound mind in a sound body."

17

Introspection vs. Meditation

There is all the difference in the world between introspection and meditation. Introspection often creates more problems than it solves; meditation always brings us inner peace.

It might be good here to define our terms. Introspection entails taking an honest look at ourselves. Meditation does the same thing, but it looks much, much deeper and puts us in touch with our essence. To put it simply, introspection gives us a relatively superficial glance at ourselves. Meditation focuses us on our true self, our God-self. Often the two terms are confused with one another. And because people are sometimes "turned off" by all this self-analysis they end up avoiding meditation like the plague.

A few years ago, I ran into a man who had been in the seminary with me many years earlier. He left the seminary during his theological studies, and is now a happily married businessman. I asked him what he was doing to grow spiritually, and he replied: "I avoid all introspection. I had enough of that in the seminary." As he spoke, he literally shuddered. What passed as meditation in the seminary was something he obviously wanted nothing to do with today.

He was so "turned off" because meditation used to be presented as taking moral inventory of oneself. If a person were in any way scrupulous or even idealistic, he or she would dread such an experience. It would frequently end up as an exercise in putting oneself down. No wonder he shuddered. That kind of introspection scares us because it puts us in a constant state of confrontation with our "shadow."

The "shadow" represents the flip side of the public image we have of ourselves. If we are striving to be decent human beings (as are the great majority of the human race), our "shadow" will confront us with everything about ourselves that is inadequate and hypocritical.

If we run into that sort of confrontation every time we begin to look within, no wonder we find a million and one excuses to avoid being alone with ourselves and God. Such a self-hatred trip is never fun and never redemptive.

In fact, concentrating on our shortcomings is the best way to start heading for depression. The classical definition of depression is anger turned against oneself. Superficial introspection usually leads us down into the pits.

Meditation is one hundred percent different. In meditation we begin with a total belief in our own inner beauty, which is God's gift to us. Even if we are not feeling very good about ourselves, we refuse to give in to feeling. We stubbornly insist on believing that our essence is love.

We do not ignore our weakness. But we insist on seeing our weakness in the context of our fundamentally beautiful spiritual identity. Then we are not so overwhelmed by all of the "not-yet-ness" about ourselves. We learn to embrace our "shadow" — the prodigal son part of us — with compassion.

Meditation puts us in touch with our essence. People who meditate tend to be peaceful because each day we focus on that which is ultimately real about ourselves.

People who are "too busy" to meditate and people who engage only in superficial introspection never have that kind of peace.

The distinction between introspection and meditation may appear to be subtle, but it is a distinction that needs to be made.

A world of people who are living on the surface of life is a scary place to be in. But a world of people meditating daily on their own inner beauty can be like heaven on earth.

Part Three

Attitudes

18

Cosmic Humility

After a talk I gave one night, a little old lady with rosary beads came up to me and asked, "Father, don't you think the problem with people today is that they have too much education?"

Without trying to sound anti-intellectual, I must admit that she has a point. We are so caught up in analyzing, dissecting, measuring, and weighing the different parts of the universe that we have forgotten how simple life is meant to be.

We cannot see the forest for the trees. We have lost sight of the big picture. We have so aggrandized the accomplishments of humankind that we can no longer see how small we really are. We need a bit of cosmic humility, some old-fashioned ego-reduction.

There is an ancient Irish prayer that goes something like this. "God, protect me; your ocean is so great and my boat is so small."

We twentieth-century moderns have forgotten how small our boat really is.

In terms of the whole sweep of evolution, for example, we represent just a grain of sand on the seashore. Put it this way: if we were to telescope the entire evolutionary process into one calendar year, it would take us until September before the first dinosaurs made their appearance. It would not be until December 24 that the first human being arrived on the scene. And recorded history would not begin until 10:30 P.M. on December 31. How is that for putting us in our place!

Or what about some perspective on the space we take up. At one time everyone, especially the Church, thought that the sun revolved around the earth. Now we find that we are not the center at all, but one of many planets revolving around our sun. In addition, we now know that there are 100 billion other suns in our galaxy. We are also certain that there are at least one billion other galaxies. And who can say that all of the galaxies we have discovered aren't like just one cell in a much larger cosmic organism?

It truly boggles the mind. God's ocean is so great and our boat is so small.

Some scientists who cannot see the forest for the trees continue to miss the big picture. But others, especially some physicists, are beginning to come out of the closet and admit their strong mystical leanings. Einstein was among the first of many such scientists. According to Dr. Fritjof Capra, "at least fifty percent of the physicists of our country are into physics because of the mysticism in it."

Some people still get nervous whenever they hear anything having to do with mystery. But a mystery is not something that is unexplainable. It is something so explainable that at any given moment you can only understand a little bit of it. In that sense many physicists are comfortable being considered mystics.

Father Matthew Fox makes an interesting observation. He notes that if Dr. Capra's observation is correct, then "there is a greater percentage of physicists who are mystics these days than priests or ministers."

The saints and mystics, contemporary physicists, and the little old ladies tolling their beads are aware of how much they do not know. Maybe we can learn from these people to be a little more humble and a little less pretentious. Our boat is very small on God's great ocean.

19

"Making Room" for God

Recently I was reviewing some of my old sermons, and I kept coming across a sentence that now rubs me the wrong way. The sentence is: "We should make room for God in our lives."

Now what could possibly be wrong with such an innocuous sounding sentence? Plenty. It is just one more way of contributing to the illusion of having an independent ego. The presumption seems to be that there is this little "I" that is gracious enough to give God a bit of room in its life. How absolutely generous of us!

Lots of people think this way. It is the classic mistake, the tragic flaw of humankind. We think that we are the center of the universe. We are blind to how small we are in the ultimate scheme of things.

Our reasoning goes something like this: I have a family and a job and lots of responsibilities. One of my responsibilities is to "make room" for God in my life. So I clear away a little time from my busy schedule and give it to God. How eminently reasonable of me.

What we need, of course, is a Copernican revolution whereby all of our assumptions are reversed. We need to allow life to radically realign our assumptions and our identity. We need a conversion whereby we discover that God is at our center and at the center of everything. Indeed, nothing has any existence apart from God. As Saint Paul put it, "It is in him that we live and move and have our being." We are not called to "make room" for God at all. We are challenged to discover the amazing fact that God is the only reality that ultimately exists. There is no "us" at all apart from God.

If it is difficult to find words to describe this transformation, it is much more difficult to undergo it. We are referring here, of course, to the conversion process. This is the shattering of all our certainties and of our very ego-structure itself. The end result is that we ultimately discover that, as Jesus said, "the kingdom of heaven is within you."

Not that many people ever go through the conversion process. They choose to remain on the surface of life and try to manipulate God. It is said that God created us in his own image and likeness and we have been returning the compliment ever since. The ego is so intent on control of reality that it even tries to control God.

This is, of course, a futile process. Ultimately, we must let go of control, at least at the moment of death. Whether we choose to end this charade of being in control early in life or at the moment of death, the point is that every human being must ultimately step into mystery. The advantage of letting go earlier in life is that we begin to taste eternity here and now.

Such individuals who have discovered the presence of transpersonal, divine energies within themselves are said to be "born again." This term is a "turn-off" to a lot of people because it has come to be associated almost exclusively with one style of spirituality. If you do not like the term, you can use the Zen Buddhist term of "waking up" or the Hindu term of "enlightenment." The name we give to the process is not all that important. What is important is that we discover our identity in God. This is a great experience and is what true religion is all about.

The simple fact of the matter is that we do not "make room" for God at all. It is God who has made room for us. How fortunate are those who can exclaim with Saint Paul: "It is no longer I who live, but Christ who lives within me."

20

Being Liked

Have you ever met anyone who did not like being liked? Probably not.

There is an inner urge within all of us to be popular and highly esteemed. This is perfectly natural. We only begin to run into difficulties when being liked by others becomes an obsession.

It is more important to be authentic than it is to be popular. As human beings with a certain sense of integrity, we are called to speak the truth as we see it. In doing so, we will not always make everyone happy.

A priest friend of mine is fond of saying that in any situation in life 25% of the people will love you no matter what, 25% will despise you no matter what, and 50% could care less about you. There is a lot of wisdom in this observation.

One of the first steps in mental and spiritual health is to get over this obsession with trying to please everyone.

In the Broadway play *Mass Appeal*, there is a marvelous portrayal of a pastor who simply cannot transcend his desire to be highly esteemed by all of his parishioners. In trying to please everyone, he ends up almost losing his soul.

When we start off with pleasing others as our main goal, we find ourselves becoming "two-faced." With one group of people we say one thing. With another group we shift gears and tell them what they want to hear. In the end we are nothing more than a split personality who does not know who he or she is.

One of the paradoxes here is that when we quit trying to please everyone and just start being true to ourselves, we actually end up being respected a lot more than the glad-handers with the plastic smiles.

A clear example of someone who was true to his convictions is Jesus. We are told in the Scriptures that Jesus was generally popular with the masses. But we also know that he was rejected by the people of his own hometown, and was high on the enemies list of the religious leaders of his day. In short, some liked Jesus and some despised him. But Jesus was not running in a popularity contest. He said what he had to say and did what he had to do for one reason only: he believed he was in touch with the voice of God within.

Like Jesus, we are called to "tune in" to the Higher Power within. Once tuned in as well as we can be, we are then expected to take a stand and let the chips fall where they may.

How can we take such a risk? Won't mistakes be made? Sure they will. But if we really believe that all of God's creation is good (including people), we can generally trust our own judgment. And even when we are wrong, the Holy Spirit will keep the world on course.

The world seems filled with wishy-washy, lukewarm, ambitious social climbers. What we need are men and women who stand for something.

Studying the history of the Church makes one fact perfectly clear. The truly great individuals have never had an easy time of it. Jesus was crucified; Francis of Assisi was thought to be crazy; Catherine of Siena was called a "loose woman"; Teresa of Avila was called proud; Thomas Merton was called an egotist — and on and on. In short, those who have been the brightest lights in the history of the Church have seldom been well-liked.

All of this is not to say that we should go out looking for trouble. It is simply to say that if we are true to our convictions, not everyone is going to like us. And that is OK.

21

Good, Better, Best

Faith does not mean buying the "party line" lock, stock, and barrel. Faith means trust. It means letting go of where we are now and allowing Christ to guide us as we move deeper into the mystery of life.

Without faith we never get out of the batter's box. It is the absolute first requirement for anyone who wishes to grow. If we cannot trust someone to guide us, then we are paralyzed and immobilized by our fears. Without faith there is no hope.

As important as faith is on our spiritual journey, there is a further step that is even better. That step is understanding. As Saint Anselm taught, understanding follows faith. First of all, we trust the guidance of Christ. Then, gradually, if we are fortunate, we gain some understanding of what we believe.

For many people, understanding is not necessary. They have a simple faith and take everything on face value. But there are many others who have inquiring minds. These individuals simply have to have some intellectual framework in which to put their religious experience.

That has certainly always been the case with me. I remember that as a freshman in high school, my religion teacher confided to my parents that she was afraid I was losing my faith. When my startled parents asked why she had such a fear, my teacher responded: "Because Thomas is always asking so many questions." The implication seemed to be that the intellect has very little importance in the religious search.

Thinking has always been important to me. Back in 1976 when I went through a full-blown religious conversion experience, I remember desperately searching for some theologian who could help me make sense out of what I was experiencing. Happily, I came across the writings of Morton Kelsey, who gave me a philosophy of the sacred. It was as crucial to me then as it is now to understand why it makes sense to believe.

There is no doubt about it. While it is good to have faith, it is even better — at least for some people — to understand what they intuitively believe. This brings us to the third and best way of religious knowing: experience.

As long as one just has faith, that faith can always be shaken. In fact, people sometimes lose their faith. When people have an understanding of what they believe, however, they are not so easily moved. But when individuals have experienced something firsthand, then they "know that they know that they know." One can never be talked out of a firsthand experience. It belongs to a person for all eternity.

When we actually experience God on this earth plane, we acquire an inner peace that belongs only to those who know their place in the ultimate scheme of things. We have been "saved." Saved from what? From absurdity, meaninglessness, guilt, games, and head trips.

In the early days of the Church, there was much more of an emphasis on experience. Catechumens were put through a training program that went on for years, and then were gradually introduced into the mysteries of Christianity. People were encouraged to feel and experience the risen Christ. These Christians had such deep inner convictions based on experience that they were willing to die for their beliefs.

In the last couple of centuries we lost sight of the value of religious experience. Now we are regaining it. The eventual result of this rediscovery will be, in my opinion, a Church made up not just of simple believers but of people for whom the Christ event is the center of their lives. I look forward to such a Church.

22

Being Real and Spiritual

One of the toughest challenges on the spiritual path is learning how to be real. The temptation is to fly off to some lofty spiritual heights and to deny or repress our own humanity.

The only authentic spiritual growth is the kind that learns to integrate the human and the divine elements within us. It is relatively easy to say "yes" to God and to deny all that is human. The real trick is to say "yes" both to God and to the human condition at the same time.

This trap of choosing between God or the world is a mistake that frequently happens to neophytes on the spiritual path. Adolescents and young adults, in particular, are capable of tremendous, heroic sacrifices for God. In their youthful idealism they are ready to give their all for God.

As beautiful and pure as this intention is, it gradually dawns on the maturing Christian that we are not called to spend our lives on the mountaintop. We are to descend the mountain, go back to the marketplace, and find God there, too.

It is no longer an either/or question. We do not choose between God and the world. We come to realize that the incredible challenge God gives us is to find God in the midst of the human drama. We are not angels, nor are we animals. We are human, and it is our unique role in evolution to become the meeting ground for the human and the divine.

This is not to say that mountaintop experiences are not important. They are. But mountaintop experiences only give us a glimpse of the final goal. Knowing what the final goal is and actually arriving there are two different things.

People who keep their eyes exclusively fixed on the final goal of life are not the kind of people you would want in a foxhole with you.

They are frequently in a dreamlike trance, spaced out, living in their own world.

There is room for such individuals in God's plan. They are prophets pointing out to us that the earth plane is not our final home. But most of us are called to roll up our shirt-sleeves and get on with the business of co-creating Planet Earth with our Creator.

Before we come to this realization, however, we often sense a need to tap into a sense of the transcendent. According to Drs. John Firman and James Vargiu, a person who is moving in this direction may "push the other aspects of the personality — such as physical needs, sexual drive, or intellectual curiosity — out of the way, ignoring them, quieting them, or even forcibly repressing and 'starving' them. The integration of the personality may then come to a stop — or may even regress."

The mistaken assumption behind this course of action is that if one can experience the transcendent intensely enough, and maintain that state indefinitely, then the individual can live the rest of his or her life in the rarified atmosphere of this new state of consciousness and ignore one's human needs. A further assumption seems to be that focusing on God is somehow more noble than dirtying our hands with the human endeavor.

There is, however, nothing second-rate or "unspiritual" about trying to find the divine within our human nature. Indeed, several monks have told me they honestly feel that people who are living "in the world" are actually responding to a more difficult challenge than those who live in monasteries.

If that is the case, then our task is not to flee from the world but to find God within it. This is always a lot trickier than turning exclusively to God and turning our backs on all that is authentically human.

23

Building the Earth

There are, I suppose, some people who have no desire to change the conditions of our world. The fat cats and wheeler-dealers are doing just fine, thank you, and don't want anyone upsetting their applecart.

But most human beings, certainly all true Christians, long for a world without nuclear weapons, without illiteracy, disease, draught, and massive starvation. The question is: How do we bring about a different kind of world, a world where all people see themselves as one family, the family of God?

At this point the cynics chime in, saying that such a world is impossible to attain. We are told that only naïve idealists think that humankind can improve its lot. The simple truth of the matter is that God has given us the power to create whatever kind of world we choose to live in.

The reason that I believe such a world is eminently within our grasp is because of the marvelous gift of change. We are not stuck with a static universe and a changeless cast of characters. No thing and no one lasts forever. All of creation is involved in an endless dance of death and rebirth.

Every second, some two and one-half million red blood cells are born in our bodies; every second, the same number dies. Every day, 15,000 babies are born on Planet Earth. Imagine, each day we get a chance to start over in teaching our children how beautiful life can be.

This brings us to the importance of good education in building up the earth.

Certainly the primary educators of these 15,000 new members of our species born each day are their parents. The values learned at home, especially during the first five years of life, are most significant.

Our school systems are then given the task of passing on knowledge and values to our youngsters. The role of the educator should never be minimized. Teilhard de Chardin looked at teachers in almost a mystical light. He called them the high priests and priestesses of the "noosphere" (the layer of thought and love encircling our globe). It is the job of teachers to pass on to the next generation the very highest of which we as a race are capable.

We Catholics handle this job in one of two ways. One option is to send our children to public schools and then give them their moral and spiritual education in parish religious education programs. The second option is to send the youngsters to Catholic school.

Theoretically, the Catholic school approach offers tremendous possibilities. In Catholic school classes the dimension of values and morality can be brought into each discipline. The false division between the secular and the sacred can be unmasked. We can feel free to talk about a holy, grace-charged universe. We can transcend political and national differences and speak about all human beings as our brothers and sisters and about the whole universe as the Body of Christ.

I began the last paragraph with the word "theoretically," because it is a fact that such an approach is not always followed. By calling itself Catholic, a school does not automatically qualify as a training ground for the Christian message. For example, do all Catholic teachers refer to the Russian people as our brothers and sisters in Christ? Do we teach our youngsters that sharing our abundance with others is not a matter of charity but of justice? How many of our high school seniors are familiar with the American Bishops' 1983 Peace Pastoral?

Certainly, we should all examine our consciences to see how we can do a better job of building a better world. We all need the gift of perspective. We think in terms of months and years. God thinks in terms of centuries and millennia.

The one thing we should never tolerate is negative, defeatist thinking. With God's guidance and our cooperation, we absolutely have it within our power to make this heaven on earth.

Part Four

Dilemmas

24

Childhood Traumas

It is difficult to overestimate the importance of a healthy childhood. Some psychologists go so far as to say that the basics of our adult personality are all set in place by the time we are five years old. Even those who would not go quite that far agree that childhood experiences play a major role in the development of our self-identity.

Much psychiatric therapy entails helping people to get in touch with repressed childhood experiences. Apparently, undealt-with trauma affects the way we presently behave, even though we would swear that we have put all those negative happenings out of our minds.

The situation of undealt-with childhood trauma is like those boats that take tourists through the lagoons of Disneyland. The boat certainly appears to be guided by the captain at the steering wheel. He is constantly checking his instruments and turning the wheel every which way. Common sense would indicate that the captain is in total control. The reality, however, is that the boat is being pulled along by a chain under the water.

Most of us are the same way. We seem to be the captain of our ship, in total control of things. In reality, however, we are not really free. We are being controlled by unconscious factors operating far beneath the surface. To become free, we need to recognize that we are still in chains.

People who never arrive at this realization go through life crippled by nameless fears, anxieties, and guilt complexes. They are not bad people by any means. It is just that they are only half-alive.

An example of such a person from the Old Testament is Isaac, the son of Abraham. As you may recall, Abraham was asked by Yahweh to sacrifice his beloved son, Isaac. Just when Abraham was about to go through with this test, Yahweh stopped him and rewarded him for his faith.

When we hear this story, we are inevitably impressed with the great faith of Abraham. But did you ever ask yourself what this experience did to Isaac? Can you imagine the trauma of a young boy seeing a knife in his father's hand, ready to be plunged into his heart?

Somehow Isaac is able to go on with life after his childhood trauma. But Isaac is much different from the other Old Testament leaders. Abraham, Moses, David, Jacob, and others were very spiritual people. They communicated with God by dreams, visions, and impassioned prayers. Not Isaac; he just followed the Law and did what he was expected to do. Perhaps he was so frightened by God during his childhood trauma that he was afraid ever to get close to God. Who could ever have love and intimacy with so fearsome a God?

Are we, then, doomed by our childhood experiences? No. Is there hope for us to break those lifelong shackles? Yes, certainly. One approach is Reality Therapy, popularized by Dr. William Glasser. In this technique, one focuses intently on the consequences of one's present activity and forgets about dredging up the past. The idea seems to be that we will never be able to eliminate the old tapes. We will, however, be able to acquire a new set of tapes and play them at a louder volume.

Such an approach, however, can be unconvincing because it lacks an explicitly spiritual basis. In my opinion, an experience of God's love is still the best medicine. When we are swept up by the love of God, our old hurts are gradually healed. We learn to forgive our parents, our teachers, and ourselves. Nothing sets us free like unconditional love.

25

The Problem of Evil

The film *Time Bandits* has been called a modern-day version of *The Wizard of Oz*. In at least one of its aspects — the way it handles the problem of evil — *Time Bandits* is even more impressive than *The Wizard of Oz*.

In *Time Bandits* Satan is portrayed as someone who is powerful but basically insecure. His insecurity stems from the fact that he has been created by God. In other words, Satan is not on an equal footing with the Creator.

This understanding of reality is based on good theology, even though many people think that Satan is stronger than he is. It is very common to run into individuals who believe that life is all about two equally strong powers — good and evil — that are warring over people's souls.

This common misunderstanding goes back to Gnosticism and Manichaeism, ancient heresies that taught that good and evil are equally powerful. Although these heresies were condemned long ago, remnants of this mentality continue to exist until the present day.

The simple fact of the matter is that God is the only ultimate reality. When creation eventually runs its course, all things will be restored in Christ. In other words, the devil is a loser. That has already been decided. Evil, which is destructive energy, will be burned away by the love of God. The victor in this game has already been decided.

Does this, then, mean that evil is — as some people believe — only the absence of good? Here one must make a technical distinction. Evil has no ontological basis, but it does have an existential existence for us here and now. Let me explain.

Only God is absolute. Only God is the foundation of being. But God permits evil here on earth as something that we have to deal with for a limited time. In other words, as the *Dictionary of Biblical Theology* puts it, "Satan, already conquered, now has only limited power; the end of time will see him and his helpers definitely vanquished."

We, however, do not live at the end of time. We live in the here and now, and so must struggle against the devil just as Jesus did. As the Letter to the Ephesians says, ". . . we are not fighting against human beings but against the wicked spiritual forces in the heavenly world, the rulers, authorities, and cosmic powers of this dark age." For us, living in the in-between times, evil is simply a reality that we cannot ignore.

What folly it is when people try to act as if there is no such thing as destructive, autonomous forces within the psyche. There are at least seven of these disordered forces that work toward the disintegration of the human person. Traditionally, they are referred to as pride, covetousness, lust, anger, gluttony, envy, and sloth.

To ignore the existence of these drives is to give them power over us. When we face our evil tendencies, protected as we are by the power of the risen Christ, they somehow lose their ability to harm us in any ultimate fashion. These forces never disappear, but at least we are able to keep them from taking over our personalities.

In considering the problem of evil there are two extremes to avoid. The one extreme is to place Satan on an equal footing with God. The other extreme is to try to lull oneself into pretending that evil is just a figment of the imagination. The Church has often emphasized how harmful it is to ignore the reality of evil. While there is merit in this approach, it seems to me that we run the risk of giving the devil more than his due. The simple yet amazing truth of things is that God is absolute. No one, not even Lucifer, is on a par with our God.

26

Spiritual Inflation

Some religious experiences can, at times, be overwhelming. We can be so filled with God's love and presence that we think we are like God. This is what is known as spiritual inflation.

In a sense, of course, we are like God. We have been swept up into the mystery of the Son. But we are not the Father, not the Source. Like Jesus, we must always remain sons and daughters of *Abba*, our Daddy.

Mental hospitals are filled with people who have not made this subtle distinction. Visit any mental ward and you will find people who are absolutely sure that they are God the Father or Jesus Christ incarnate.

People who think this way are probably closer to the Truth than those sick souls who think that God is utterly removed from them. After all, we are called to share in the life of the Trinity, not just observe it from afar. But our calling is to participate in God's life, not usurp it.

Like Icarus from Greek mythology, some try to fly so close to the sun that they are burned in the process. We are called to accept and glory in our humanity. To flee from our humanity — to wish to be an angel or to try to play God — can get us in a lot of trouble.

One of the best examples of what can happen when we forget our places in life comes from Walt Disney's movie *Fantasia*. In the story, Mickey Mouse plays the Sorcerer's Apprentice. It is Mickey's job to go and fetch water for the Sorcerer. But Mickey is tired of carrying buckets of water. If only he can get hold of the Sorcerer's magic hat, he will never have to work again.

One day when the Sorcerer is gone, Mickey gets his chance. The Sorcerer has gone off and has left his magic hat behind. Mickey puts on the magic hat and commands the broom to carry the water for him. It works. So far, so good.

Mickey sits in the Sorcerer's chair and contentedly falls asleep. He then has a dream about the ocean with waves rising higher and higher. When he wakes up, he sees that that is exactly what has happened. The broom filled up the basin with water, but then continued to bring in so much water that the cavern is almost filled with it.

Mickey did not bargain on this happening. "Stop, broom!" he cries, but the broom keeps right on with its work. Now Mickey grabs an ax and hacks the broom into a hundred pieces. But then, before his eyes, each splinter of wood becomes a full-sized broom with arms and legs, and begins to bring in more water.

Now Mickey is in a panic. He has lost control. Just then the Sorcerer reappears and, with one wave of his arm, restores the cavern to its previous condition. Suddenly remembering that he is still wearing the magic hat, Mickey returns it to the tolerant Sorcerer.

Chastised, Mickey realizes how foolish he was to pretend to be a sorcerer. He returns to being a water carrier again. He now realizes his place and has come to accept it.

On the spiritual journey, this scenario happens more often than most people realize. Especially in the initial stages of conversion, people sometimes think that they have it all together. There is frequently smugness about a recently born-again Christian, for example, that is a real "turn-off" to others.

The individual thinks that he or she knows all the magic spells. Usually, such spiritual neophytes end up over their heads soon enough. They discover that their magic spells work only so far and that they themselves are not the person with all the answers.

Humbled, they gladly go back to being a water carrier once again.

27

Impossible Situations

Recently, I received a letter asking me to address a very complicated issue:

If one is living in an "impossible" situation, isn't it sometimes better to just give up and leave?

The writer mentions the examples of being married to an alcoholic or a compulsive gambler who uses the family's money for his or her own addiction. How can one still be peaceful when bill collectors are constantly calling and mortgage companies are threatening to foreclose? Isn't it better in such situations to just throw in the towel and leave?

First of all, it is crucial that we try not to allow external circumstances to control our happiness. If we are subject to mood swings every time someone around us is having a bad day, we will have very few special days. The goal is to find one's center and to operate from that space in every situation. Ultimately, we are all responsible for our own happiness or depression. No one does it to us. We do it to ourselves.

The late Father Jack Villano used to spend hours trying to convince me of that point. As only he could say it, he would insist that we "sick" ourselves or "health" ourselves. He would ask me, "How are you doing yourself these days?" His point was to get me to accept complete responsibility for my own happiness and quit trying to blame or credit others with my happiness or unhappiness.

Finally, he got through to me. I was at last able to "own" my feelings and take responsibility for my state of mind. In fact, I even began to give talks about positive thinking and the need to control one's destiny.

Then the Lord played a practical joke on me. I found myself in an impossible situation. Try as I might, use all the positive thinking that I could muster, still I found myself unable to cope.

First, I "depressed" myself. The classical definition of depression is anger turned against the self. My self-esteem was hurt because I could not hang in there, so I got angry at myself.

Finally, I had to accept my inability to cope. Without blaming anyone, I simply had to come to terms with the fact that I could not hack it anymore in that situation.

This was a very important lesson to learn. Before learning it, I might have glibly and self-righteously advised people to try to persevere in any situation. In fact, I may have tried to lay a guilt trip on them by insisting that we are the sole determinant of our happiness. My advice would now be tempered by personal experience. What I learned the hard way is that each situation is unique and each person has to do what he or she has to do.

For example, some marriages have their share of difficulties, but the relationships at least are not destructive. It is possible to hang in there for the good of the children and for other reasons. But some marriage relationships are destructive. No one — including the children — is being helped by living in a hateful situation.

It is the same with rectory or convent situations. Such a lifestyle is, in my opinion, somewhat unnatural or at least artificial. You just cannot throw together a group of people with different backgrounds and expect everything to turn out smoothly at all times. By mutual acceptance and mutual respect people in such situations can often learn to "make a go" of it. But sometimes things simply do not work out.

As psychologist Leo Buscaglia says, life is a stage and sometimes we need to change the actors. Sure, we are ultimately responsible for our own happiness. But taking responsibility for our own happiness means that sometimes we simply have to move on.

28

Dying to Self

One of the most misunderstood aspects of the spiritual path has to do with self-denial.

Perceived properly, self-denial can set us free to enjoy life with more gusto than we ever thought possible. Misunderstood, it can mess up our minds with self-rejection and self-hatred.

When we are born, we are fundamentally beautiful. On the seventh day, God saw everything that he made and it was good. This includes us.

There is, however, a certain tendency for all of us to lose sight of our original splendor. We lose sight of the God within and fall into the great illusion that we are someone apart from God. When we live with such blindness we can never be happy. Eventually, we grow frustrated with living "the great lie." It is at such a moment that we are now ready to discover the Higher Power within us.

There is only one difficulty with this. To discover the kingdom of heaven within us, we have to temporarily leave the ego behind. Jesus speaks of this process as "dying to self." In no way is he trying to imply that there is something fundamentally wrong with our essence. Our essence comes from God and is absolutely perfect. Jesus is referring, instead, to the artificial construct of the ego. It is that aspect of ourselves that must undergo a kind of death.

All of the false gods of the ego must be sacrificed temporarily in order to discover the kingdom within. The sacrifice must be total. To find God we must be willing to "let go" of whatever we are addicted to: food, drink, sex, sports, motherhood, fatherhood, our jobs, everything.

Don't panic. Just as God intervened before Abraham sacrificed Isaac, so God never takes the good things of our life from us. We are not asked to reject anything that is authentically human. It is just that we must be willing to hold nothing back from God. We must be willing to consecrate absolutely everything.

For some, the process of dying to self is a relatively smooth one. They have about twenty-five mini-crises a week instead of one or two "biggies." The rough parts of the human personality are chipped away gradually. Such folks are known as "smooth evolvers."

Most of us, however, need to have the bottom fall out of our lives before we get moving. At such times, the ego does not have any answers. The person is forced to pray from the soles of his or her feet upward. We are out of our depth, out of control, and in need of a lot more than rationalizations and human cleverness. We then cry out to God from the depths of our being.

At this point, it often seems that our worst fears may be realized. We have "died" to all our past securities; we have trusted in God; and we still feel abandoned by God. Was it a mistake to have even begun the spiritual journey? we ask ourselves.

At such a time we feel a little bit like the Israelites who left the relative comfort of Egypt in pursuit of the Promised Land. Moses promised them milk and honey, and all they see is sand and all they feel is thirst. The Israelites wandered in the desert for forty years. Although our period of disillusionment might not be quite that long, it often feels like it is.

But if we can hang in there and trust the process, we eventually get to drink from the "living water" within us. Then our sacrifice and our trust is rewarded. Everything we were willing to "give up" is given back to us. All of our past pleasures are now more enjoyable since they are experienced as gifts rather than compulsions.

Dying to self may be painful, but its ultimate payoff is pleasurable. For when we discover the God within, all of life is divine.

29

True Leisure

Some people have to discipline themselves to work. Like many Americans, however, I must discipline myself to slow down.

At first glance, this seems strange. After all, aren't we all inherently lazy? Wouldn't we love to have the time to just goof off? Isn't it the burning desire of every spiritual seeker to "waste" time with the Lord? Apparently not. Most of us do not have the slightest idea how to relax.

Some people are out-and-out workaholics. They are married to their jobs. They are not free *not* to work. They push and push themselves beyond all reasonable limits. Such individuals do what they do because of enormous personal insecurity. They are always trying to please, to win, to conquer.

The above example is all too common. Most of us, however, are not quite so compulsive. After all, don't we look forward eagerly to our weekends and our vacations?

It is true that we are indeed happy to have some free time. But do we slow down at all during these opportunities? Not really. We fill up our free time with different types of activities. It never dawns on us to try doing nothing at all. Instead, we plan every single moment of our free time with one activity after another.

Some are into competitive, organized sports. Others love to travel and see new things. Still others prefer to work around the house or to read novels. But how many of us have ever learned to do nothing at all? The word "vacation" comes from the Latin word *vacare*, to make empty. The idea is to clean the slate, stop our dictatorial, rational mind, and simply be in the present.

To do nothing is not laziness. It is a positive effort to face reality as it is, to open the floodgates of creativity, and tune in to the voice of God within.

Most people are scared to death of doing nothing. We find it disconcerting to be alone for even a few hours. We are enormously threatened by the prospect of spending a whole day by ourselves. People are so afraid of true leisure because we prefer to live in a world of our own making. As long as we are on the go and interacting with others and bombarded by noise and distraction, then we feel in control.

When we are doing nothing, then we begin to see reality as it is and — most frightening of all — we begin to see ourselves as we are. The shallowness and inconsistencies of our lives begin to come to the surface. We come to terms with our pomposity and our pride. It is not easy to be by oneself and to do nothing.

Because we are unwilling to bear the pain of self-confrontation, we jump back headlong into a life of senseless and ultimately unhappy activity. This frenetic pace is taking its toll. Every day we as a nation consume eighty million Valium tablets. We are so uptight we are ready to burst.

What we fail to realize is that true leisure is well worth the personal cost. Facing the junk in our lives is the first step to true inner peace. After we face it, we can let it go and begin to get in touch with the springs of living water inside ourselves. For some this will take place in the context of a formal retreat. For others, it could mean learning to give ourselves some space during our vacations that does not have to be filled with planned activity. Others might try to just stop thinking and scheming long enough to stop and smell the roses.

It is time for all of us to stop our robotlike behavior and begin to be human beings again.

Part Five

Directions

30

We're Still the One

In these days of ecumenism it is not fashionable to sing the praises of one's own religion. But, darn it, I just can't get over what a good thing we have going for us.

Religions always seem to go to extremes. Some religions tend to stress the "otherness" of God. Some religions, on the other hand, insist that God is not "out there" at all: God is within. Catholic Christianity strikes the perfect balance between the two extremes. That is why it is the "best" religion.

The religions stressing the "otherness" of God paint him as inaccessible, wholly removed from human nature and the human situation. Such religions feel that it is impossible to ever grow close to God. The only way to reach God is to go forth from one's normal self at death.

The above mentality accords with what William James called the "sick soul." It is a mentality which leads to extreme forms of penitence and self-abasement, since it is appalled by the extreme contrast between itself and the Perfect which it contemplates.

Such a "sick soul" tends to be extremely pessimistic, tending as it does to be overly sensitive to the elements of evil and imperfection in itself and in the entire human situation. Such a soul conceives of the material world and itself as being infinitely far from God.

That caricature of religion is the one held by Karl Marx and many of the great intellects of our time. Clearly, it is inadequate for them. Happily, it is inadequate for the true Christian also.

But its opposite extreme, the God "within," can be equally erroneous and unhealthy. Viewed in its extreme, this theory of God seems to offer good news to an alienated, guilt-ridden human race. It implies that the quest for the Absolute is nothing more than the realization of something which is already within oneself. God is not "out there" at all; he is really found within me.

It all sounds so good. What could possibly be wrong with such a "liberating" way of viewing reality? The difficulty is that if one finds God only within oneself, one can tend to identify with God himself. Our mental hospitals are full of such psychotics who are convinced that they are God the Father or Jesus Christ.

Both of these extreme but all too common forms of religion are inadequate. That is where Christianity comes in.

It is the perfect religion, not because it offers a compromise between the extremes, but because it contains the best elements of both. We are able to let God be God while we come to the marvelous conclusion that he truly dwells in our souls.

When we enter into the Christ-life, God himself truly "divinizes" us. He takes up his dwelling place within us, while still remaining "Wholly Other." Christianity offers a happy tension between the "outside" and "inside" God. We adore him "out there," but he is within us, more intimate to us than we are to ourselves.

The balanced Christian relates to God in this way. And it was the opinion of psychologist Carl Jung that the Catholic brand of Christianity contains the most profound set of symbols ever devised to foster mental health and put one in touch with God. By this set of symbols Catholics become aware that God is greater than they, yet discover that the "kingdom of heaven" is within.

Catholics can more easily go deep within the depth of their consciousness and there find buried in their souls that "spark" spoken of by Eckhart, that "ground" spoken of by Tauler, that Inward Light spoken of by the Quakers, that Divine Principle spoken of by the Transcendentalists.

With all this, Catholics avoid schizophrenia because they look into themselves, not to escape from reality but to truly find it.

Our religion has made it for 2,000 years because, with all of its human error and sin, it still tells it exactly like it is.

31

Vows for All

Analyze any organization in the world and you will invariably find the same three games being played: the money game, the sex game, and the power game. All three games tend to dull the soul and, if taken to an extreme, make spiritual growth difficult.

The Church wisely understands the intensity of these three basic human drives. Consequently, those who are serious about the spiritual journey are encouraged to embrace the three vows of poverty, chastity, and obedience. This is done to try to counteract these drives.

It seems to me that all Christians ought to give serious consideration to observing the spirit of the vows. We might live them out differently than monks and nuns do, to be sure, but the vows seem too important to be monopolized by those living a formal religious life.

Poverty, for example, obviously implies more than just an absence of material possessions. Real poverty comes when we share ourselves with others. On the other hand, we do seem to have lost sight of the value of simple life-styles. In the United States, for example, there are more than a million millionaires.

The drive to always have "a little more" runs very deep inside us. I heard an old priest say that when he was younger his greatest temptations had to do with sensuality. Later, he had to wrestle with tendencies to rebel against authority. Finally, as an old priest, he felt driven to hoard money and possessions. He sees avarice as the most deadly drive he has ever had to deal with.

Chastity does not imply sexual repression but, rather, emotional sincerity. To assert otherwise would mean that marital love is unchaste, an obvious absurdity.

Married couples, then, should constantly seek to integrate their sex into the context of spiritual love. In that way lovemaking becomes more than just an occasion for a release of sexual tension but, potentially, a spiritual experience.

The *drive to power* is perhaps the most insidious drive that exists. It is an ever-present reality that everyone — single, celibate, or married — must deal with. Obviously, power can be used constructively for the good of others. The only difficulty is that it usually does not seem to work out that way.

Any business or organization can tell all sorts of horror stories about how people will knife others in the back in order to get ahead. Everyone wants to be one rung higher than the other guy.

Office buildings are even constructed that way. New employees get offices on the lower floors. As one progresses up the corporate ladder, the offices are on progressively higher floors, eventually terminating with the president sitting on top of everyone in his penthouse suite.

One reason people strive so hard for power is that they are unable to express themselves creatively. As José Arguelles puts it, "When a man is deprived of the power of expression, he will express himself in a drive for power."

Some men who experience little power at their jobs decide to play "little Caesar" at home. They yell at their wives, who will either yell back or take it out on the kids. The kids have to do something to exert their power, so they kick the dog.

People in the world of business are not the only ones who have troubles with power. Clerics play the power game as well as anyone. In the clerical life-style, creativity is discouraged, innovation is a no-no, even new ideas are frowned on. Is it any wonder that so many play a clerical version of the Nixonian "I am the President" game? Clerics may not go to bed with women, but a lot go to bed with power.

The way I see it, poverty, chastity, and obedience are for all Christians. Those three vows were not picked out of the sky. They represent an attempt to deal with the three most fundamental drives that we human beings have to face.

32

Holy Russia

For centuries Russia produced many holy men and women. In fact, the Church nicknamed it "Holy Russia."

Then came the Revolution. The Church was virtually shut down, and it seemed as though "Holy Russia" had lost its faith overnight. A country of mystics had turned into a country of agnostics in a couple of decades. Incredible.

What has puzzled me about all this is my belief that the spiritual impulse is innate in human beings. How can people, then, lose their spirituality as a result of political edict? How could the state have been so effective in legislating away people's faith?

Here we must make a distinction between religion and spirituality. Religion has to do with dogmas, rites, rituals, and moral codes. Spirituality has to do with people's attempts to reach God. It is possible for a religious person not to be very spiritual. And it is possible for a spiritual person not to be very religious.

In Russia, the state was able effectively to eliminate religion. But, we are finding out, it was not so successful in suppressing the Russian spiritual impulse.

The state had such an easy time in debunking religion because the Church bureaucracy had "sold out" to the ruling class centuries ago. The Church had allied itself with the czar for self-protective reasons. When the Revolution came, the Church was seen as an arm of the state. Heads rolled, and the Church was closed down tightly.

By the way, one of the real strengths of the American Church is that it opted long ago to identify itself with the poor. In Russia this was not the case at all. Consequently, the Church as an institution quickly went the way of the czar.

The fact that religion has disappeared from the Russian scene in no way implies that these fiercely spiritual people have lost their mystical impulse. In fact, according to Michael Murphy, who recently visited Russia extensively, the Russian people are on the verge of a new kind of revolution — a spiritual one.

Murphy is best known as the founder of Esalen, one of the best-known human consciousness centers in the world. Because of his extensive international contacts, he was able to get beyond the organized tours and propaganda packages prepared by the Soviet government. He got to meet thousands of Russians in their homes, and he reports a spiritual ground swell taking place.

Murphy reports, first of all, an intense interest in spiritual healing. In fact, a woman healer named Jhuna is reported to have worked with the late Leonid Brezhnev. It is a fact that this healer has met with 350 members of the Soviet Attorney General's staff and has conducted workshops all around Moscow.

Komonsol Pravda, a newspaper for young people, with a circulation of eleven million, recently proposed the founding of a national institute for spiritual healing. Predictably, *Literaturnaya Gazeta,* the Soviet literacy gazette, downplayed the idea as a return to superstition. But the fact it was proposed says a lot.

In addition, Russians are becoming interested in homeotherapy, acupuncture, psychic healing, biofeedback, physiological self-control, and herbal medicine. They are dabbling in clairvoyance and telekinesis. They are forming encounter and Gestalt groups, meditation circles, Gurdjieff groups, and parapsychology clubs. They are reading *Life After Life,* Raymond Moody's best-selling book on near-death experiences. They are also reading books by Fritz Perls, Carlos Castaneda, John Lilly, and Abraham Maslow. They are studying Eastern religions, Jewish mysticism, and the lost knowledge of ancient civilizations.

About the only thing they are not studying is Christian mysticism. Given their history, that is understandable. But, with time, that too will come to pass.

All of this just goes to show that God has created us as spiritual beings. It is, therefore, impossible to suppress the human quest for spiritual meaning. What is happening in "Holy Russia" today demonstrates that point with great clarity.

33

Science and Religion — At It Again

Science and religion are at it again. The latest episode in the age-old battle between science and religion has just come to an end. As usual, nobody won.

The most recent skirmish took place at an unlikely location called Star Island. Present were over 100 big shots from Harvard, Penn, and other prominent places of learning. What made this conference somewhat unique was that the theologians present did not dispute the scientific findings. They merely insisted that science was incapable of measuring the theologians' most important piece of data: the religious experience of millions of ordinary people.

Let us backtrack a bit. The conference was called to discuss why people believe in God. The scientists were all excited; they had just discovered that people believe in God because the human brain is programmed to believe that way. They figured that this bit of data would send the theologians scrambling. Instead, the theologians asked one salient question: "Who did the programming?"

The scientists were not at all thrown off by this retort. Their response was the highly questionable thesis that the human race programmed its own brains to believe. Millenia ago, according to this claim, people had such a fear of reality that they created the idea of God.

This is a totally gratuitous assumption. It cannot be proved. And it is not automatically correct just because some scientists would like it to be correct. But just for the sake of argument, let us say it is true. We are still faced with a situation that even the scientists admit is a dead-end street: we have an unchangeable need to believe in God.

Psychologist Carl Jung had a lot to say on this matter. It was his learned conclusion that we are stuck with this need to believe in God whether we want to or not. Jung said that his research convinced him that no one can be happy unless he or she acts as if God exists.

Jung was a Christian. He also happened to believe that God exists. But he was careful to not let his personal beliefs get in the way of his scientific detachment. He insisted that the need to believe in God can be demonstrated on purely psychological grounds. For good mental health, we simply must give in to this basic drive.

Based on the insights of Dr. Jung and others, the theologians at Star Island were able to handle easily every argument advanced by the scientists. But then the theologians took the initiative. They asked the scientists to explain the consistently similar religious experiences of so many people throughout the world.

It is one thing to say that people have an *idea* of God. It is something else entirely to say that people today actually *experience* God.

Sociologist Andrew Greeley has uncovered an amazing fact. When protected by the cloak of anonymity, a high percentage of average Americans admitted that they have had moving religious experiences. Prior to the survey, many of them had told no one about the experiences, especially their local clergymen. But the fact remains that millions of people walking the streets have had firsthand experiential knowledge of the sacred.

When presented with this fact, one of the scientists cynically asked how many of those present had ever had such experiences. When well over half of those present raised their hands, the crestfallen scientists quietly acquiesced.

When the conference was over, probably no one changed sides. When you are speaking about religion or politics, people seldom do. But the 200-year-old assault of science on the spiritual is slowing up a bit. The scientific community is becoming more humble. It is slowly coming to realize that, by itself, it will never have all of the answers to the riddle of life.

34

Physics and Spirituality

We live in an age of convergence. Rather than remaining in enemy camps, the major disciplines of the world — science, psychology, and spirituality — are all in the process of arriving at the same conclusions.

Perhaps the most exciting reunion is the coming together of physics and spirituality.

The old Newtonian physics that most of us learned in school is now outdated. In outer space, gravity no longer applies. With atomic fission, two objects colliding do not necessarily bounce off one another. They "implode." Most pertinent of all, we no longer believe that anything is solid.

Solidity is an optical illusion. In reality, nothing is solid. Everything is energy; everything is in constant motion; nothing ever remains the same. If we were to take any seemingly solid object and put it under a high-powered enough microscope, we would find that it is teeming with energy. There are protons and neutrons and electrons swirling about in a cosmic dance.

For modern physics, what we call matter is nothing more than energy with a certain mass to it. According to Einstein, primal energy has rearranged itself millions and millions of times, taking on new shapes in each incarnation.

Does this kind of talk sound more mystical than scientific? If it does, that is because modern-day physicists are some of the most spiritual people around. Einstein himself had a strong belief in God. Most physicists since the turn of the century have had the same sentiments. Their research is revealing to them that the mystics of the great religions of the world were right on target after all.

In Hinduism, the great god Shiva is portrayed as half male, half female, both creating and destroying, as Shiva dances in perpetual motion. This is a symbolical way of stating that the basic life-force is both masculine and feminine, eternally creating new life as present manifestations decay and return to the Void.

In Christianity, of course, we speak of the dynamic motion of the Spirit. We believe in this primal energy that comes forth from the Godhead and eternally begets new life as the universe evolves to Christ-consciousness.

With a change of vocabulary here or there, most contemporary physicists would have no trouble in accepting both the Hindu and Christian world views.

What the great spiritualities have always insisted upon is that the ultimate reality is Spirit. Dependence on material reality is a foolish mistake, for all so-called material things decay and perish. The only ultimate reality is God.

Material goods and creatures are at the service of Spirit. They are to be "used" reverently and never to be made a false idol in life. The wise person is the one who enjoys life without trying to hold on to it. We can even let go of our loved ones as they return to the Mind of God.

Once again, this is religious language that describes precisely the world view of a twentieth-century physicist.

One of the most articulate spokespersons about this convergence of physics and spirituality is physicist Fritjof Capra. In 1977, Capra wrote *The Tao of Physics*, a book which has become a mini-classic for New Age thinkers. His latest book, *The Turning Point: Science, Society and the Rising Culture*, has already received rave reviews. In *The Turning Point* Capra shows the implications of living in a new world based on Spirit and love for the universe. It is dynamite stuff.

People journeying in the Spirit have often had to maintain their beliefs while being mocked by the scientific community. But that is no longer the case. Science and spirituality have not just stopped bickering, they are getting ready to tie the knot.

35

Spiritual Director

The very term *spiritual director* evokes an image of one person directing another person to do something. This idea of spiritual direction is seen today as being out of date. I would like to propose ten images of spiritual direction that are more in line with contemporary thinking on the matter. Here are the images.

1. *Companion.* A companion may be leading you on the journey, but this person is by no means a spectator. You are journeying together.

2. *Soul friend.* We all have need of friends who share various levels of intimacy with us. But a "soul friend" is someone special. This is someone to whom and with whom we can share the hidden secrets of our hearts. Having a soul friend demands a very deep level of trust. We are opening up to such an individual at the deepest levels of who we are.

3. *Guide.* A guide is simply someone who has been there before and who understands the terrain. There is no moral superiority or intellectual one-upmanship implied. The guide knows the traps and pitfalls from experience. With an experienced guide we are provided with a road map and some practical pointers.

4. *Midwife.* This is my favorite image. The director is aiding the spiritual birthing process of the directee. With this model the directee already has the truth within. It just has to be brought out into the light of day. The midwife cooperates with nature and, once the baby has been born, the midwife fades into the background.

5. *Spiritual friend.* The best part about this image is that it highlights the fact that one does not have to be a professional to do the job. In fact, be a bit wary of people who "hang out their shingle" as licensed, certified professionals in the field. Good direction can come from a brother or sister in the Lord who acts as

a sounding board for us to articulate the deepest yearnings of our hearts.

6. *Prophet.* Even though the relationship has a high degree of mutuality to it, sometimes the Spirit may prompt the director to challenge his or her soul friend. In other words, a good director is not afraid, in a loving way, to confront. Very little is accomplished by always telling people what they want to hear.

7. *Physician of the soul.* While the director does not have to be professionally trained, some knowledge of psychology as well as some background in the history of spirituality can be of immense help. Whether trained or not, however, the director is accepting some responsibility for the health of the person's soul. In that sense, this image has some validity.

8. *Leader of mountain-climbing expedition.* While all of us must journey up the mountain by ourselves, we are wise to have a leader. The leader knows the "ropes" and all of the nooks and crannies of the mountain. The leader puts the guide ropes in place, gives us encouragement, and shows us by example that we can keep climbing a little higher.

9. *Spiritual counselor.* The problem with this image is that it is too detached. It conjures up the image of a stuffy academic type impassionately doling out tidbits of wisdom. Some still prefer the term, however.

10. *Lightning rod.* The lightning rod attracts energy to itself. It brings down power from the heavens and grounds it safely to the earth. This is precisely what a good director does. He or she takes in spiritual energy and makes it available to normal people.

None of these images is completely adequate by itself. Some are complementary, while some appear to contradict others. That is because we can never put God in a neat little box, and we can never find the precise words to describe the divine-human encounter.

36

Room for All Types

Each part of life can tell us something about the big picture. Even something as small as a cell can shed light upon the meaning of life.

We now know that there are three different actions taking place in the life of a cell.

The first has to do with the cell's "memory." This function is interested in maintaining continuity with the past. It lets the cell "know" where it has come from and what its purpose is.

The second thing happening in a cell is a movement by which the cell functions efficiently in the here and now. Something tells the cell how to do its job smoothly and effectively.

Finally, there is a tendency in each cell to look toward future adaptations. All currently existing life forms have had to make many changes over the last five billion years in order to be alive today.

What do these three tendencies of the cell teach us? They teach us that within all of us there are three separate movements: a part that maintains contact with the past, a part that focuses on how to be most effective in the present, and a part that looks toward future possibilities.

Furthermore, since the Body of Christ is a living organism, there are individuals who correspond to each of these three tendencies of a human cell.

There are, first of all, some individuals who seem to specialize in embodying the wisdom of the past. This part of the Church is extremely important because religious delusions are always right around the corner on the spiritual journey. These traditional individuals keep us rooted in reality. They help us avoid the tendency for each generation to reinvent the wheel. Without the presence of traditional types, we could very easily go off the deep end and further splinter the Body of Christ.

There are other members of the Body who have the gift of getting things done in the real world. These are the movers and shakers who pay the bills, execute programs, and make the presence of the Church credible to the community at large.

In addition, there are others who have been gifted with the ability to see further possibilities. These are the visionaries who say, like George Bernard Shaw, "Some see things as they are and say why, I dream things as they never were and say why not."

For a cell to be vital, all three tendencies must be there: contact with the past, healthy functioning in the present, and openness to adaptation in the future. For the Body of Christ to be vital, we need all three types of individuals, too.

Unfortunately, there is a tendency not to recognize and affirm the various gifts. Individuals have presented our choices as either/or rather than both/and. As a result there has been polarization in the Church, and we have all suffered a bit from it.

Those with the gift of keeping us in contact with our spiritual roots have played a dominant role in the recent life of the Church. But it is also time to start utilizing the tremendous talents of those who have the ability to make the Church more credible today. We currently have the resources to set the world on fire with the life of the Spirit if we use the gifts that the Church already has. And, of course, it is important for us to recognize the prophets among us. Prophets always make us uncomfortable. But without them the Church would fast become just an ancient relic of the past.

In short, we have room for all types in the Church. A cell absolutely needs contact with the past, effective functioning in the present, and adaptation to the future. The Church needs no less.

37

Two or Three

Everyday thinking seems to indicate that a small group of people cannot make much of a difference in the world. The latest research on the matter, however, indicates just the opposite.

This latest insight comes from a scientific theory called "formative causation." According to this hypothesis, a change in the thinking of one or two members of a species somehow changes the consciousness of the entire species.

For example, monkeys on an island near Japan were introduced to a new food: freshly dug potatoes covered with sand and grit. The other food that the monkeys ate was clean and needed no preparation, so they were reluctant to eat the dirt-covered potatoes. Finally, one monkey genius figured out how to wash the potatoes in the stream, and she taught a few others how to do it. Then an astounding thing happened. At a certain point, a change of consciousness took place in the entire monkey population. Even those monkeys on the other side of the island, who had not been taught to wash potatoes, somehow intuitively knew what had to be done. Apparently, the "thought field" of the entire monkey population had been changed by the breakthrough of a few monkey geniuses.

Although it was now clear that the consciousness of all the monkeys on the island had changed, the researchers were absolutely shocked when they discovered monkeys *on another island* beginning to wash dirty potatoes in clear water. Apparently, the change in learned behavior and the change in consciousness of the two test monkeys had effected a change upon a large group of the entire species.

People with the deepest insight into Christianity have always believed basically the same thing about human behavior. We have always believed, in our finer moments, that a few spiritually attuned individuals could change the spiritual atmosphere of whole geographical areas.

That is why wise bishops have traditionally coveted the presence of contemplative congregations in their respective dioceses. A few individuals deeply tuned in to the Spirit can have repercussions upon millions of people.

If this is the case, then just think of the impact that a couple of praying people can have upon a smaller geographical area like a parish. Without necessarily getting involved at the front lines, two or three people can potentially effect revolutionary changes upon the thinking of those whom they love.

An example of this kind of service was provided by a group of Transcendental Meditation people in Atlanta, Georgia. On three separate occasions, TM groups went and meditated in areas that had a high incidence of violent crimes. On all three occasions, the crime rate dropped dramatically.

The two social psychologists who conducted this experiment concede that crime rates vary in the same area from week to week. However, given the consistent eighteen-to-thirty-percent reduction in crime each time the group went in, the social scientists feel that "the probability is almost nil that these results happened by chance."

I have no particular ax to grind with Transcendental Meditation, but meditation that is not spiritually grounded simply cannot be as powerful and safe as Christian meditation. If the TM people could have those kinds of results in Atlanta, what are the possibilities for a few people praying for a community in the name of the risen Christ?

Jesus taught us: "Whenever two or three are gathered together in my name, I am there in their midst." We simply do not have to worry about playing the numbers game. A couple of individuals plugged into the Spirit are capable of changing the spiritual consciousness of a parish or an entire diocese.

Suggested Reading

Part One: Beliefs

Morton Kelsey. *The Other Side of Silence: A Guide to Christian Meditation.* Paulist Press, 1976. Paperback.

Part Two: Behavior

Maxwell Maltz, M.D., F.I.C.S. *Psycho-Cybernetics.* Pocket Books. Paperback.

Part Three: Attitudes

Robert Muller. *New Genesis: Shaping a Global Spirituality.* Doubleday, 1982. Paperback.

Part Four: Dilemmas

John Sanford. *Healing and Wholeness.* Paulist Press, 1977. Paperback.

Part Five: Directions

Fritjof Capra. *The Turning Point: Science, Society and the Rising Culture.* Bantam, 1984. Paperback.

OTHER TITLES FROM LIGUORI PUBLICATIONS

INNER CALM
A Christian Answer to Modern Stress
by Dr. Paul DeBlassie III

Combines modern psychology with spirituality to help readers discover greater peace and joy through the centuries-old method of meditation known as the "Jesus Prayer." Contains a wealth of healing experiences and offers a way to find true inner calm in today's world. $3.95

BECOMING A NEW PERSON
Twelve Steps to Christian Growth
by Philip St. Romain

Presents twelve practical steps to help you break free in your Christian life, to develop a healthy self-love and acceptance of personal strengths and limitations. An aid to becoming a better you, a happier you — a new person. $2.95

DARE TO BE CHRISTIAN
Developing a Social Conscience
by Bernard Häring, C.SS.R.

This different look at the whole idea of "holiness" can help you become "light to the world." It presents a simple invitation to see Christ by seeing the problems of others, to reach Christ by reaching out to others, to love Christ by loving others. $4.25

IN PURSUIT OF HOLINESS
by Bernard Häring, C.SS.R.

This book offers wisdom, spiritual direction, and a sense of prayer. It shows how to discover holiness in yourself and the people you meet. $2.95

60 WAYS TO LET YOURSELF GROW
by Martha Mary McGaw, CSJ

Upbeat and joyous, this journal-type book shows how to make the most out of life. Each page presents an idea or suggestion to help the reader grow — and includes free space for personal notes. $1.50

Order from your local bookstore or write to:
Liguori Publications, Box 060, Liguori, Missouri 63057
(Please add 50¢ for postage and handling for the first item ordered and 25¢ for each additional item.)